Student Book

Mary Roulston and Mark Roulston

Contents

UNIT 1 — Why do we invent?

Reading 1	Factual text: Accidental Inventions	Page 6
Reading 2	Fiction: Here We Come!	Page 12

UNIT 2 — How can we learn about history?

Reading 1	Fiction: The House of the Jaguar	Page 22
Reading 2	Factual text: New Technologies in Archeology	Page 28

UNIT 3 — Why do we move to new places?

Reading 1	Factual text: Moving on	Page 38
Reading 2	Fiction: Big Apple, Small World	Page 44

UNIT 4 — How do we stay safe?

Reading 1	Factual text: Saving and Delivering Lives	Page 54
Reading 2	Fiction: The Boy Who Cried "Fire"	Page 60

UNIT 5 — Why do we protect animals?

Reading 1	Factual text: Endangered Animals	Page 70
Reading 2	Fiction: Pollinators and Pandora's Box	Page 76

UNIT 6 — What's literature?

Reading 1	Factual text: What Do You Feel Like Reading?	Page 86
Reading 2	Fiction: Eyes in the Dark	Page 92

UNIT 7 — How do we communicate?

Reading 1	Factual text: Digital Detox	Page 102
Reading 2	Fiction: Head Boy Hearing	Page 108

UNIT 8 — How are things made by hand?

Reading 1	Fiction: The Blue Ribbon	Page 118
Reading 2	Factual text: Claudia's Bird Board	Page 124

UNIT 9 — Why do we play sports?

Reading 1	Factual text: Extreme Limits	Page 134
Reading 2	Fiction: Come On, Grandpa!	Page 140

UNIT 10 — What's causing extreme weather?

Reading 1	Factual text: Ask a Scientist!	Page 150
Reading 2	Fiction: Trapped!	Page 156

UNIT 11 — Why do we cook?

Reading 1	Factual text: What's Cooking?	Page 166
Reading 2	Fiction: Stone Soup (from China), Axe Soup (from Russia)	Page 172

UNIT 12 — How do we learn?

Reading 1	Fiction: A Surprising Test, The Day of the Exam	Page 182
Reading 2	Factual text: Memory Tips from the Masters	Page 188

Listening
- I can recognize linking words/phrases signaling the sequence of events.
- I can understand details in extended dialogs.

Reading
- I can understand details in longer texts.
- I can follow extended texts.

Speaking
- I can give an opinion in a structured discussion.
- I can talk about past activities.

Writing
- I can write descriptions of personal experiences.

1 💬 Look at the picture and discuss.

1. What inventions can you see?
2. How do you think each of these inventions changed people's lives?
3. What's the most important invention in your house? Why?

2 💬 Read and make notes. Then compare your answers with a friend.

1. Do you think inventing things is easy or difficult? Why?
2. Are all inventions complicated?
3. What new invention has been created since you were born?

3 ▶ 1-1 BBC Look at the video still and predict. Where would you find a motor like this?

4 ▶ 1-1 BBC Watch the video and check your answer from Activity 3. Then watch again and circle T (true) or F (false).

1. The car looks futuristic. T F
2. The motor is very small. T F
3. The car is powered by batteries. T F
4. The batteries powering the motor are in the floor of the car. T F

5

Pre-reading 1

1 Think about something you have created. Discuss with a friend.

1. What was your initial idea?
2. What steps did you follow to create it?
3. Did it turn out as planned?

📖 Reading strategy

Use information in a historical, scientific, or technical text to explain ideas and procedures.

2 Read. What was the idea? What was the procedure?

I wanted to make a quadcopter. I drew the four **blades** on styrofoam and cut them out. I glued a small motor on each blade and then glued them to a styrofoam ball. Next, I attached propellers to each motor and connected the **wiring** to batteries. It worked … but not very well.

3 🎧 1-02 Read *Accidental Inventions*. What were the inventors' original ideas?

Reading 1

Accidental Inventions

Microwave Oven

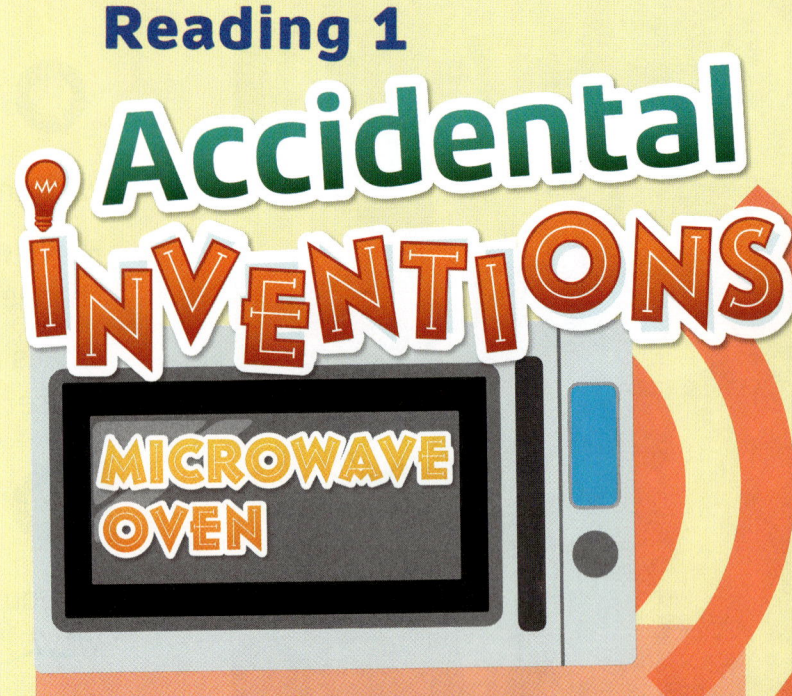

In 1946, the engineer Percy Spencer wanted to find a new use for the **radar magnetron**, a machine which generated the microwaves for radar systems. Spencer was next to the device one day, and a chocolate bar in his pocket **melted**. Spencer ran another test with the magnetron. This time he put an egg underneath the tube. Moments later, it **exploded**! The next day, Percy Spencer brought in corn kernels, popped them with his new invention, and shared some popcorn with the entire office. The **microwave oven** was born.

POTATO CHIPS

George Crum was a fantastic chef, who worked at a hotel in New York State, U.S.A. In 1853, a cranky guest complained about Crum's fried potatoes. The guest said that they were too thick and **soggy**, and demanded a new batch.

Crum was upset. He decided to play a trick on the diner. The chef sliced a potato paper-thin, fried it until a fork could shatter it, and then put too much salt on his new creation. He thought the diner would hate the potatoes. But the man loved them! He ordered some more.

Word of this new snack spread quickly and it became a hit across New England, and Crum went on to open his own restaurant. Today, that accidental invention has become a massive snack industry.

PLASTIC

Plastic is all around us. How many plastic things can you see in your classroom? Leo Baekeland was a Belgian chemist. In 1907, he created the first plastic but probably did not set out to fill the world with it. He wanted to find a replacement for shellac, a resin made by a South Asian scale bug! People used this resin as varnish.

Shellac is still very popular today as nail varnish!

Baekeland made something new by mixing chemicals, but it didn't work as a shellac substitute. He put the mixture in a big iron cooker. Then he **heated** it. After that, he mixed it with wood flour. This created a material that was mouldable but strong. He called his invention *Bakelite*. He said it was "the material of 1,000 uses."

Since then, Bakelite and other new plastics have changed the stuff that our world is made of. There's a negative side to this invention, however. Most plastics will remain in the environment for centuries, if not thousands of years. We've replaced materials that are timeless with one that simply lasts a really long time.

Bakelite was used to make **electronic** components, **car parts**, cameras, telephones, **buttons**, clocks, radios, toys, **kitchenware**, chess pieces, and tens of thousands of other items.

4 Which accidental invention do you think has been the most successful?

5 What are the negative impacts of plastic and the other inventions? Discuss with a friend.

Comprehension 1

1 Match the inventor to the ideas and the inventions.

Inventor	He was trying to ...	He invented ...
1 George Crum	find a replacement for shellac	microwave oven
2 Leo Baekeland	play a trick on a cranky guest	potato chips
3 Percy Spencer	find a new use for the radar magnetron	plastic

2 Read *Accidental Inventions* again and write *PS* (Percy Spencer), *GC* (George Crum), and/or *LB* (Leo Baekeland). Some items have more than one answer.

He ...
1 cooked food. ....
2 combined chemicals. ....
3 was a cook. ....
4 created a kind of oven. ....
5 was an engineer. ....
6 invented something we still use today. ....

Listening 1

3 What new invention can you think of that would make your life better? Discuss with a friend.

Listening strategy
Listen for words indicating steps in a procedure.

4 🎧 1-03 Listen. Who uses Glo-Sheets?

5 🎧 1-04 Listen again and complete. What words introduce a step in a procedure?

.... → .... → .... → ....

8

Vocabulary 1

1 Find these words in *Accidental Inventions*. Then write them in the correct category.

🇬🇧 British	🇺🇸 American
car part	auto part

> auto part   blade   button   electronic   explode   heat
> kitchenware   melt   microwave oven   radar   soggy   wiring

1 This is a machine. ....
2 These are action words. ....
3 You use it to fasten your clothes. ....
4 These are used in machines. ....
5 This is a word for all the machines and tools in the kitchen. ....
6 This is an adjective that means *soft and wet*. ....
7 This adjective means *involving computers*. ....
8 This system uses radio waves to find objects. ....

2 🎧 Listen and say.
1-05

3 💬 Work with a friend. Choose one of the inventions from *Accidental Inventions* and tell your friend about it using some of the words from Activity 1.

4 Look at the word families and complete the chart.

Person	Noun	Adjective	Verb
inventor		inventive	
	engine		engineer
			create
	conduction		

5 💬 Think about something that could work better or faster. How would you improve it? Discuss with a friend.

Grammar 1

1   Watch Part 1 of the story video. Read and complete.

Mom isn't very happy. Mr. Perkins .... her about my little accident with the rocket. At first, Mom .... very angry.

2  Watch Part 1 of the story video again. How did Jade and her mom get home?

3 Read the grammar box and complete.

> **Grammar**
>
> **1 Past Simple regular verbs**
> You add **-ed** (heat**ed**) or **-d** (explode**d**) to regular verbs to make Past Simple.
>
> **2 Past Simple irregular verbs**
> For irregular verbs, for example **have**, **go**, **do**, **run**, and **say**, we don't use -ed. What are their Past Simple forms?
> ....
>
> **3 Past Simple to be**
> The verb **be** is the only verb to have more than one Past Simple form. It has two forms.
> They are: I/he/she/it .... ; you/we/they ....

4 Read *Accidental Inventions* again and complete the sentences.

1 Spencer .... another test with the magnetron.
2 Moments later, it .... !
3 A chocolate bar in his pocket .... !
4 The guest .... the potatoes were too soggy.
5 Crum .... the diner would hate the potatoes.
6 After that, Baekeland .... the chemicals with wood flour.

5 What did you do in your English class last year? Discuss with a friend. Then write.

1. What did you learn?
2. What topics did you discuss?
3. What characters did you watch in the videos?
4. What stories did you read?
5. What was your favorite thing?

6 Watch Part 2 of the story video. What did Ms. Philips show the friends?

Speaking 1

7 Look at the word cloud. Which verbs do you think are the most commonly used in English?

Speaking strategy
Show that you are listening to your friend's ideas.

9 Do a survey to find the most popular answers to question 5 from Activity 5.
- The class is divided in two.
- Ask everyone in your group the question and record the answers.
- Think of an interesting way to present your results.

What was your favorite thing last year?

I liked the videos.

8 A word cloud is one way of presenting information. What other ways could this data be presented? Discuss with a friend.

11

Pre-reading 2

1 Think about your favorite book. Discuss with a friend. Can they guess the book?

1 What's it about?
2 Give a short summary of the story.

Reading strategy
Summarize a text.

2 Read. What do you think is the theme of the story?

Last Days on Earth

My mom is running around like a crazy woman. She wants to make sure we don't forget to pack anything important. Dad is still doing last-minute checks to his machine at the laboratory. He invented a machine that will create rainfall on Mars. Now our whole family is relocating 54.6 million kilometers. Being an inventor's daughter has some big implications!

3 🎧 1-06 Read *Here We Come!*. What's the theme of the story? Summarize the story with a friend.

Reading 2
HERE WE COME!

Grandma sat beside Lyla on her bed. Lyla looked sadly out of the window at a night sky full of stars. "Tell me about when you were my age, Gran," said Lyla, "Tell me about your first robot."

"OK," said Grandma, "it was the year 2025, and I was 10, like you are now. My family was one of the last to get a robot, so I was really excited. It didn't have legs, it had **wheels**, and a **screen** for a face. It could **rotate** its head 360 degrees!"

"So, it didn't look like a **human**?" asked Lyla.
"No, not like they do these days," said Grandma. "It was an electronic device, but it was very **basic**. It had some **Artificial Intelligence** like voice recognition. It could follow our orders, do housework, and drive the car. My parents loved it! We called it Robert – get it? Robot/Robert."
"Oh, Grandma – even the jokes weren't as good in the past!" groaned Lyla.

"Don't complain about the past, look at where we are now!" exclaimed Grandma.

"I know," said Lyla, turning serious again. "What happened to Robert?"

"He malfunctioned after about ten years. We had to replace Robert with a new home help robot called M1A, we called her Mia. She was completely different from Robert: no screen, no wheels. She had arms, legs, and a face – she looked far more like a human than something **mechanical**. We couldn't believe that she was an electronic device made of circuit boards and wiring."

"Was that where it all started?" asked Lyla.

"I guess so," said Grandma. "The companies that **developed** robots were competing to be the first to create true A.I. It was **complicated**, so it happened slowly. They didn't realize how **risky** it was."

"Well, they succeeded," said Lyla, gloomily.

"Look on the bright side," said Grandma, "at the same time other engineers were working on supersonic space travel, and they succeeded, too."

"I know," said Lyla, looking out of the window again. "But I'll miss planet Earth. And I miss you."

"I miss you, too," said Grandma, "but I'm needed here for now, and we're going to fly out to join you soon. Now get some sleep, you'll arrive tomorrow."

"Yes, I know, night-night, Grandma."

With that, Lyla turned off the **hologram** generator and her Grandma disappeared. She pressed her face against the window.

To the left she saw the bright shining star which was all she could see of planet Earth. She thought about how the robots with A.I. were controlling the whole planet except for a few safe islands. She thought about the **courageous** people who stayed to try and defeat the robots.

She turned her head and looked straight ahead and saw all the other space ships making the same journey as her.

Her dad entered the cabin with her little brother, already in his pajamas.

"How are you feeling, Ly?" he asked.

"I'm excited now," she said, smiling.

"Great," said Dad.

Lyla looked out of the window again and this time looked right. The huge red planet looked so near now.

"Mars, here we come!" she thought.

4 Why are Lyla and her family traveling to Mars? What is A.I.? What did it do?

Comprehension 2

1 🎧 1-07 Listen to Erica and Milo talking about stories. Who's talking about *Here We Come!*?

2 Read *Here We Come!* again. Circle **T** (true) or **F** (false).

1 The story is set in 2025. **T F**
2 Lyla and her grandma are in the same place. **T F**
3 Grandma's first robot was called Robert. **T F**
4 Robots have caused problems on Earth. **T F**
5 Lyla feels happy about leaving Earth. **T F**
6 Supersonic space travel hasn't been invented. **T F**

3 💬 Work in three groups and think about the story *Here We Come!*.

1 **Group A:** brainstorm ideas for how Lyla's story continues.

 Group B: brainstorm ideas for how Grandma's story continues.

 Group C: brainstorm ideas for how the robots took over the world.

2 After the first group stage, change groups. Now work in groups of three with one student from A, one from B, and one from C. Share your ideas. Which story idea do you like the best?

Listening 2

4 💬 How would you feel if you had to move to Mars? Discuss with a friend.

🎧 Listening strategy
Make inferences from details in a text.

5 🎧 1-08 Listen. Whose story does the narrative continue? Listen again and answer.

1 Who is Grandma? ....

2 Who do you think she's in command of? ....

3 What kind of ships do you think the robots are on? ....

4 What do you think the virus will do? ....

14

Vocabulary 2

1 Find these words in *Here We Come!*. Write them next to their definitions. Then write definitions for the remaining words.

> Artificial Intelligence   basic   complicated   courageous   develop
> hologram   human   mechanical   risky   rotate   screen   wheel

1 .... : **(noun)** an image created with photographic projection
2 .... : **(adjective)** dangerous or hazardous
3 .... : **(adjective)** simple, fundamental; easy to use
4 .... : **(adjective)** to do with machinery
5 .... : **(verb)** to bring out the capabilities or possibilities of something; bring to a more advanced or effective state; to grow or expand
6 .... : **(adjective)** difficult to analyze, explain; complex
7 .... : ....
8 .... : ....
9 .... : ....
10 .... : ....
11 .... : ....
12 .... : ....

2 🎧 1-09 Listen, check your answers, and say.

3 💬 Work in groups. Make a story chain using the words from this lesson.

The robot rotated its head …

… and projected a hologram from a screen.

Grammar 2

1   Watch Part 1 of the story video again. Did Jade's mom let her go out in the evening?

🇬🇧 British	🇺🇸 American
take the rubbish out	take out the trash
tidy my bedroom	clean my bedroom

2 Read and complete. Which things did Jade have to do to make Mom happy? Add two more things to each list.

> clean her room   do her homework   feed the cat
> make dinner   take out the trash   wash the car

Jade had to …	Jade didn't have to …

3 Read the grammar box and complete.

Grammar

Obligations in the past
I **had to** do my homework.
She **didn't** _____ feed the cat.
_____ you **have to** wash the car?

Ability in the past
We _____ do our homework.
They **couldn't** feed the cat.
_____ you wash the car?

4 Read *Here We Come!* again. Circle sentences with obligations or ability in the past.

5 Read and complete. Use the correct form of *could* or *have to*.

1 When I was two, I .... read or write.
2 She .... go out last night because she .... help her mom.
3 .... you .... do your math homework yesterday?
  I did, but it was so hard I .... do it.
4 When I was a baby, I had a swing that I .... bounce in.
5 My dad .... drive, so my mom .... do all the driving.

6 Think about an electronic or mechanical toy you had when you were younger. Complete the sentences.

My Toy

My favorite **mechanical / electronic** toy when I was younger was ....
It could ....
It couldn't ....
To turn it on, you had to ....

Speaking 2

7 Think about what you could or couldn't do and what you had to or didn't have to do when you were five. Discuss with a friend.

I couldn't swim when I was five.

I could swim, but I couldn't dive.

I didn't have to do homework when I was five.

Lucky you! I had to do homework!

8 Now work with another friend and discuss your ideas from Activity 7.

Writing

1 Scan Salma's blog entry. Answer the questions.

1. Is she writing about the past, the present, or the future?
2. What invention changed her life?

2 Read and check your answers from Activity 1.

The Invention That Changed My Life

| HOME | PHOTOS | SOCIAL MEDIA |

When I was little, I got a very serious disease called meningitis. I survived, but the doctors had to remove one of my legs. I could do most things that other kids could do. I went to school, I learned to walk, and I could swim. My family didn't treat me differently – I had to help at home just like my brothers and sister!

The one thing I couldn't do was run and so I couldn't play sports. I could walk on my regular prosthetic, but it was no good for running. Then, when I was six, I got my first running blades! They were invented in the 1970s. The inventor, Van Phillips, was an amputee and an engineer; he worked on developing running blades for many years.

With my running blade I could run as fast as the other kids in my class. I joined an athletics club, and now I train with other amputee kids and able-bodied kids. I want to be a Paralympic champion!

3 Read the blog again. Circle all the verbs in Past Simple.

4 Think about an invention, an idea, or an experience you had in the past that changed your life. Then go to the Workbook to do the writing activity.

Writing strategy

Use Past Simple to write about personal experiences.
*I **cycled** all the way home as quickly as I could.*

18

Now I Know

1 Why do we invent? Look back through Unit 1, remember what you learned, and write.

We invent to create new machines.
....
....
....
....

2 Choose a project.

Plan, design, and create an invention.

1. Think of something you can invent.
2. Draw your design and label it.
3. Make your invention.
4. Present your invention to the class.

or

Research a famous invention.

1. Use books and the internet to research a famous invention.
2. Find or draw pictures of it.
3. Write about it.
4. Present your research to the class.

Self-assessment

Check (✔) or cross (✘) for you.

| ✘ I can't do this yet. | ✔ I can do this. | ✔✔ I liked doing this. |

I can recognize linking words/phrases signaling the sequence of events. ☐

I can understand details in extended dialogs. ☐

I can understand details in longer texts. ☐

I can follow extended texts. ☐

I can give an opinion in a structured discussion. ☐

I can talk about past activities. ☐

I can write descriptions of personal experiences. ☐

2

How can we learn about history?

Listening
- I can identify the main points of factual talks.

Reading
- I can infer information.
- I can understand problem/solution relationships.

Speaking
- I can describe past events, using descriptive language to add interest.

Writing
- I can narrate a historical event.

1 💬 Look at the picture and discuss.

1. What are the people doing?
2. What do you think they've discovered?
3. Do you know any archeological sites close to where you live? What has been discovered there?

2 ▶ 2-1 BBC Look at the video still and predict. What are Isabel and her grandfather talking about?

3 ▶ 2-1 BBC Watch the video and check your answer from Activity 2. Then watch again and answer the questions.

1. How did Isabel's grandfather get to school?

    ....

2. How did his classroom differ from Isabel's classroom today? Write three differences.

    ....

    ....

    ....

3. How did the air raids affect the school?

    ....

4. What's the air-raid shelter now?

    ....

21

Pre-reading 1

1 Read and write in your notebook.

1 Write a few sentences describing what you did on the weekend.
2 Read them to a friend. Write a narrative of your friend's weekend.
3 Compare the two narratives of the weekend.

> **Reading strategy**
>
> Compare and contrast points of view from which a story is narrated.

2 Read. Is this a first- or a third-person narrative?

> It was hot in the midday sun. I walked to the temple with the rest of the nobles. We had walked a long way to get there, and my clothes were hot and heavy. My gold pendant was burning against my skin. I turned and saw a young boy, no older than 16, under a tree. I felt such sadness for him. Our eyes met for a moment, and then my companions rushed me inside.

3 Read *The House of the Jaguar*. Is the story told in the first or third person?

Reading 1

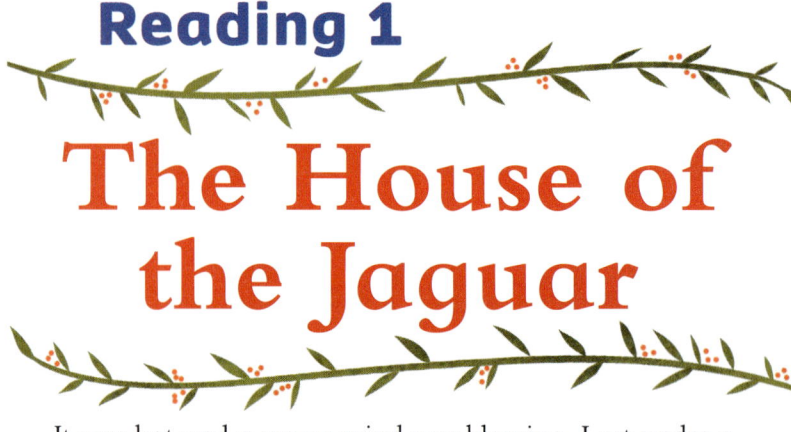

The House of the Jaguar

It was hot and a warm wind was blowing. I sat under a tree to keep cool, watching the **entrance** to the temple of our **ancestors**. I wanted to be in the cool temple air, but the guards would never let me in.

I was a peasant, a poor villager with no hope for the future. I worked on my parents' farm, doing hard work in the sun. I really wanted to be a craftsman, to create beautiful artwork and sculptures. But my parents were poor and couldn't afford for me to learn. I had to work.

Today, though, I had run away to watch the **nobles** entering the temple for a special ceremony. They were starting to arrive now, their **precious stones** glinting in the sun.

They were chatting and laughing as they walked into the temple. I saw a noble woman looking at me as she passed. I wondered what she thought of seeing someone so poor.

I thought of my mother. She would be wondering where I was. Should I go back? No, I was already in trouble. A little longer couldn't hurt. I saw a lump of **clay** and a piece of **bone** lying under my tree. To **occupy** my mind, I started moulding the clay with my hands and adding details with the bone. I moulded the clay into the form of a jaguar. I remembered the time I silently watched a jaguar while I was **labouring** one day. It was so graceful as it stalked through the trees. As I was moulding the clay, I forgot all of my troubles.

I was finishing my clay jaguar when temple guards came up to me. What had I done? They pulled me roughly to my feet. They were shouting at me, telling me I had to leave, when one of them noticed the jaguar sculpture lying beside me. He picked it up and looked at it with great admiration. He muttered something to one of the other guards and then hurried back to the temple with my clay jaguar. I was worried what this would mean for me. I should never have come here.

I looked up and saw the master craftsman striding out of the temple **exit** and towards me. He had a big smile on his face. He ordered the guards to take me to the nobles of the temple. Me, inside the temple! Could it be true? They explained that they were planning a magnificent carved **frieze** in the temple **chambers** and wanted me to join their team of craftsmen. I couldn't believe it. In that moment, my life changed forever – all thanks to my clay jaguar.

When I told my parents that evening, their anger turned to joy. The money I would make as a craftsman would mean they didn't have to work so hard. The next day I began working as a craftsman. I walked proudly into the temple.

Nearly 2,000 years later, a group of historians headed up by Mexican archaeologist Florentino García Cruz rediscovered Balamkú. **Looters** had taken many artefacts, but García Cruz and his team found part of the incredible Universe Frieze that has made this site famous. Balamkú means *The House of the Jaguar*. It's named after the amazing jaguar in the centre of the frieze.

4 What other amazing art did ancient civilizations create?

Comprehension 1

1 💬 Read *The House of the Jaguar* again. Then discuss the answers with a friend.

1. Why did the boy sculpt a jaguar?
2. Why did the guard go back to the temple when he saw the boy's jaguar?
3. What do you think is the connection between the last paragraph and the rest of the story?

2 Imagine you are Florentino García Cruz and write three sentences in your journal about your discovery. Use the first person.

3 Who wrote each narrative? Read and write *García Cruz* or *The boy*.

1. *We discovered a trench made by the looters. We started exploring the site and soon realized we had found a very important Mayan site.* ....

2. *I still couldn't quite believe the events of the previous day. When the master craftsman saw the jaguar I'd made out of clay, he thought I had a true talent.* ....

Listening 1

4 💬 Have you visited any amazing ancient buildings? Discuss with a friend.

> 🎧 **Listening strategy**
> Follow the main points of short talks on a subject that you know.

5 🎧 1-11 Listen, choose, and write. Where's each child from? What site do they live close to?

> Pyramids of Giza   Stonehenge
> The Tomb of Qin Shi Huang

1. country: ....
   site: ....

2. country: ....
   site: ....

3. country: ....
   site: ....

6 💬 What famous archeological sites are in your country? Compare and contrast them with the sites from Activity 5. Discuss with a friend.

Vocabulary 1

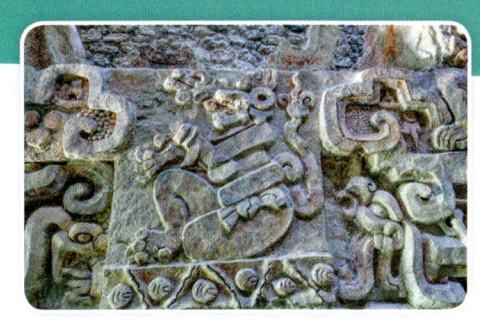

1 Find these words in *The House of the Jaguar*. Then write them in the correct category.

> ancestor   bone   chamber   clay   entrance   exit
> frieze   labor   looter   noble   occupy   precious stones

Materials

Features of a building

People

Verbs

🇬🇧 British	🇺🇸 American
archaeologist	archeologist
labour	labor

2 Work in pairs. Choose six words from Activity 1. Write definitions.

1 ....
2 ....
3 ....
4 ....
5 ....
6 ....

3 Swap your definitions from Activity 2 with another pair. Can you guess the words?

4 Imagine you've discovered an ancient site. Describe it in detail to a friend.

1 What does it look like?
2 Does it have chambers?
3 What materials were used to build it?
4 Are there any signs that looters have been there?

Grammar 1

1   Watch Part 1 of the story video. Why is Oli in trouble? Read and complete.

We .... to Mr Perkins in our history lesson.

It .... dark in the classroom ... .

2 Read the grammar box and circle.

3 Look at the sentences from Activity 1. Read and circle.

1 Jade is talking about the **past** / **present** / **future**.

2 Jade is describing a **short** / **longer** event in the past.

> **Grammar**
>
> **Setting the scene**
>
> We use **Past Simple** *to be* + **adjectives** and the **Past Progressive** to set the scene and describe background events. Circle each verb in these sentences:
>
> It **was hot** and a warm wind **was blowing**.
> It **was quiet** in the library and everyone **was reading**.

4 Look and write two sentences to set the scene. Compare with a friend.

It was a dark night.
The moon was shining.

Speaking 1

5 Think and complete the mind maps.

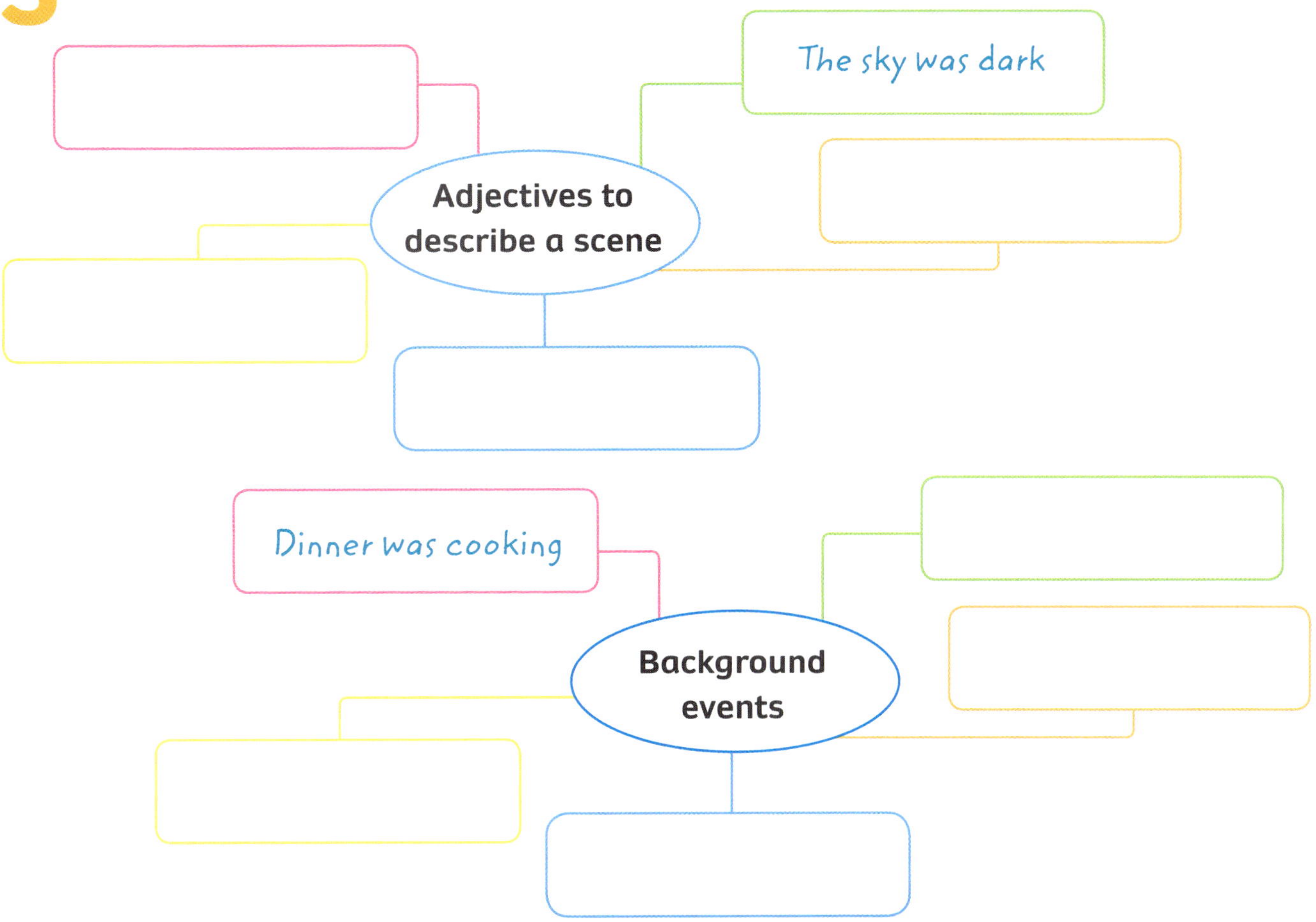

- Adjectives to describe a scene
  - The sky was dark

- Background events
  - Dinner was cooking

6 Play *Never Ending Scene-setting* in groups.

1 Take turns saying a sentence to set a scene. Use ideas from your mind maps.
2 Keep going until someone repeats a sentence or pauses.
3 Start a new scene. Use a stopwatch and see which group can keep setting a scene for the longest time!

It was a sunny day ...

... and children were playing ...

... and the birds were singing ...

Pre-reading 2

1 Think about a problem you had recently. Discuss with a friend.

1. What was the problem?
2. How did you solve it?

> **Reading strategy**
>
> Explain procedures based on specific information in the text.

2 Read. What was the problem? What was the solution?

THE ROSETTA STONE

The ancient Egyptians had a writing system called hieroglyphics. Archeologists knew that hieroglyphics would tell them a lot about the ancient Egyptian civilization, but they couldn't read them! French soldiers found a stone in 1799 which had writing on it in three different languages including ancient Egyptian and ancient Greek. This stone, called the Rosetta Stone, was the key to translating hieroglyphics.

3 Read *New Technologies in Archeology*. Why is archeology using new technologies?

Reading 2

NEW TECHNOLOGIES IN ARCHEOLOGY

What do you imagine when you think of an archeologist's job? Your answer probably depends on whether you watch TV documentaries or play video games and watch **adventure** movies! In the first case, you may imagine a team of historians on hands and knees **excavating** tombs with tiny brushes. In the second, an action hero could be running through a dark cave. But what is it really like? We meet real-life archeologist, Sara Bailey, to find out that there's a lot more to it than just digging.

> *Hi Sara, thanks for talking to us. What is it like being an archeologist? Do you do a lot of digging?*
>
> We do quite a bit of digging, yes. However, we use new technology as well. I spend a lot of time in front of a computer these days.
>
> *What do you use the computer for?*
>
> We use it to find potential **sites** of interest. Satellite images such as the ones on Google Earth have made it possible to zoom into any part of the globe to find sites. We can **spot** things like **settlement** mounds, which show where people may have lived in the past.

28

And then you start digging?

Not yet! Another technology that is helping us is called *light detection and ranging* (LiDAR). It creates a 3D map of the earth's surface by using laser beams pointed at the ground from an airplane. The laser beams produce data for the system to create the image. Researchers use LiDAR to find **ancient** sites that are covered by earth or plants.

That sounds really cool! What happens next?

We take pictures of the possible sites to **analyze**. We use drones to take pictures from the air. Before that, archeologists used things like homemade kites, helium balloons, and model planes. Can you imagine trying to operate a camera on a kite?! Drones are great because they can take pictures in low light and in poor weather conditions. Both conditions are fantastic for spotting potential **buried** sites. In future, it will be possible to mount LiDAR directly onto drones.

Drones taking pictures of potential sites

Please tell me you start digging now!

Yes, if the site looks good, we go there and get digging. And we can get our ray guns out, too.

Ray guns? Really?!

Yes. In the past, we had to send soil samples to the lab to analyze. While we were waiting for the results, we wasted a lot of time. Now we have an X-ray gun that can record samples at the site. This is great for letting us know whether there was any form of **civilization** at the site in the past, especially if there are not many **artifacts** left behind.

How else do you use modern technology?

We use it to find out how old things are. In the past, it was difficult to know the age of artifacts. Scientists were looking for better ways of dating artifacts when they discovered carbon dating. This technique can estimate the age of **remains** by measuring their carbon content. It doesn't work for **fossils** more than 60,000 years old. For fossils less than 60,000 years old, it can give rough ages within a 200-year range.

Thanks for talking to us, Sara. Now we know that archeology is a mixture of adventure, cool technology, AND digging!

4 Which type of technology do you think is the most useful? Why?

Comprehension 2

1 Read *New Technologies in Archeology* again. Number the technologies in the order in which they are used.

.... X-ray guns
.... drones
.... carbon dating
.... LiDAR
.... satellite imagery

2 Read Sara's blog and complete.

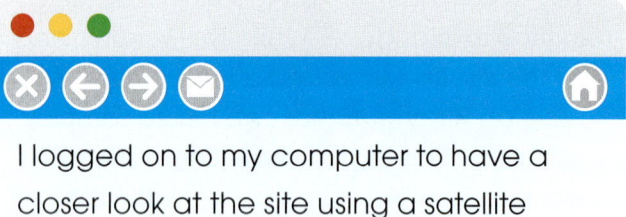

I logged on to my computer to have a closer look at the site using a satellite ¹ .... program. I zoomed in on the area. It was covered in thick vegetation, so I commissioned an airplane to map it using ² .... The scan showed something worth investigating.

A few weeks later we arrived in the area. We sent out ³ .... with cameras attached to find the exact spot. We took soil samples and used our ⁴ .... guns to analyze them. We found some artifacts and sent some to the lab for ⁵ .... to find out how old they were.

3  What would you like best about being an archeologist? Discuss with a friend.

Listening 2

4 Who is your favorite writer? Discuss with a friend.

🎧 **Listening strategy**
Listen for cause and effect.

5 🎧 1-13 Listen. What does Terry Deary do?

6 🎧 1-14 Listen again. Complete the cause and effect graphic.

1 | **Cause** | → | **Effect** Terry didn't like school.

2 | **Cause** | → | **Effect** Terry wrote *Horrible Histories*.

3 | **Cause** | → | **Effect** Terry's books interest kids around the world.

Vocabulary 2

1 Find these words in *New Technologies in Archeology*. Write a definition for each one in your own words.

adventure (n) .... ☐   excavate (v) .... ☐
analyze (v) .... ☐   fossil (n) .... ☐
ancient (adj) .... ☐   remains (n) .... ☐
artifact (n) .... ☐   settlement (n) .... ☐
buried (adj) .... ☐   site (n) .... ☐
civilization (n) .... ☐   spot (v) .... ☐

2 Look at Activity 1. How did you figure out the meaning of each word? Number the techniques you used.

1 I already knew the word.
2 It's similar to a word in my own language.
3 I used the context.
4 I used the pictures.
5 I used a dictionary.

3 Look at the words. Write *N* (noun), *V* (verb), or *A* (adjective). Then write another form of each as indicated.

1 adventure   N | adventurous   (adj)
2 analyze ___ | _____ (n)
3 buried ___ | _____ (v)
4 civilization ___ | _____ (adj)
5 excavate ___ | _____ (n)
6 fossils ___ | _____ (adj)
7 remains ___ | _____ (v)
8 settlement ___ | _____ (v)

4 💬 Do you think we can learn things from ancient civilizations? How were their lives different from and similar to our own? Discuss with a friend.

31

Grammar 2

1  Watch Part 2 of the story video. Read and complete.

Jade was helping Mr. Perkins to clean .... when she found ....

2   Watch Part 2 of the story video again. Whose picture was on Mr. Perkins's desk? What was Oli's money for?

3 Read the grammar box. Then look at the sentence in Activity 1 and answer the questions.

1 Which action took longer?
2 Which tense is used for the long action?
3 Was the long action still happening when the other events happened?

> **Grammar**
>
> We use **Past Progressive** to talk about long actions in the past.
> We use **Past Simple** to talk about short events that happened during, or interrupted, the longer action.
> I **was sitting** in the shade of the tree when one woman **stopped** and **looked** at me.
>
> We use *while* before the longer action:
> **While** the archeologists were excavating the site, they found a hidden chamber.
>
> We use *when* to introduce the shorter action:
> The kids were playing on the beach **when** the storm started.
>
> We never use *when* and *while* in the same sentence.

4 Read New *Technologies in Archeology* again. Circle sentences with Past Progressive and Past Simple with *while* or *when*.

5 Look at the pictures. Write sentences with *when* for the shorter actions.

1. ....
....
....

2. ....
....
....

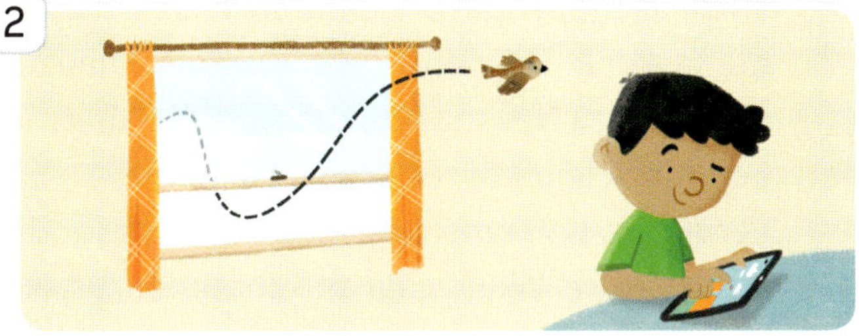

3. ....
....
....

6 Rewrite the sentences from Activity 5. Use *while*.

1 ....
2 ....
3 ....

Speaking 2

7 Play a game in groups.

> **Speaking strategy**
>
> Encourage others to tell you their story by nodding, showing surprise, and interest.

1 Write verbs on pieces of paper or card. Put the verbs cards face down.
2 Take turns picking four or more cards.
3 Start a story using the verbs. Make sentences using the verbs in Past Progressive and Past Simple, linking with *when* or *while*.

I was singing a song when I found a cookie ...

33

Writing

1 Scan the presentation. Answer the questions.

2 Read and check your answers from Activity 1.

1. Which country is the writer from?
2. What archeological site is the presentation about?

Ciudad Perdida, an Archeological Site from my Country

The ancient people of Colombia were called the Tayrona. They built over 200 settlements in the Sierra Nevada mountains of Northern Colombia. Looters rediscovered Ciudad Perdida in 1972 when they were looking for lost treasure. When gold and ceramic artifacts from this city began appearing in the local black market, archeologists decided to find the site themselves and completed reconstruction between 1976-1982.

Visiting the Site

Ciudad Perdida consists of 169 terraces carved into the mountainside, a network of tiled roads, and several small circular plazas. You can only access the entrance by climbing up 1,200 stone steps through dense jungle! I really want to visit Ciudad Perdida one day, but it's a 44-kilometer trek to get there. I have to wait until I'm older.

3 Read the presentation again. Answer the questions.

1. Is the first slide written in the past or present? Why?
2. Is the second slide written in the past or present? Why?

Writing strategy

Use a variety of verb tenses to combine historical accounts, present situations, and personal opinion.
*The Parthenon **was built** by the ancient Greeks. It**'s** my favorite building.*

4  Think about and research an archeological site in your country. Then go to the Workbook to do the writing activity.

Now I Know

1 How can we learn about history? Look back through Unit 2, remember what you learned, and write.

....
....
....
....

2 Choose a project.

Make a model of a famous archeological site.

1 Choose an archeological site.
2 Make a design and choose your materials.
3 Make your model.
4 Create a class display and give museum tours.

or

Plan an archeological adventure.

1 Make a list of what you will take.
2 Create a map detailing where you're going to go.
3 Write what you expect to find there.
4 Present your adventure to the class.

Self-assessment

Check (✔) or cross (✘) for you.

| ✘ I can't do this yet. | ✔ I can do this. | ✔✔ I liked doing this. |

I can identify the main points of factual talks.

I can infer information.

I can understand problem/solution relationships.

I can describe past events, using descriptive language to add interest.

I can narrate a historical event.

35

3

Why do we move to new places?

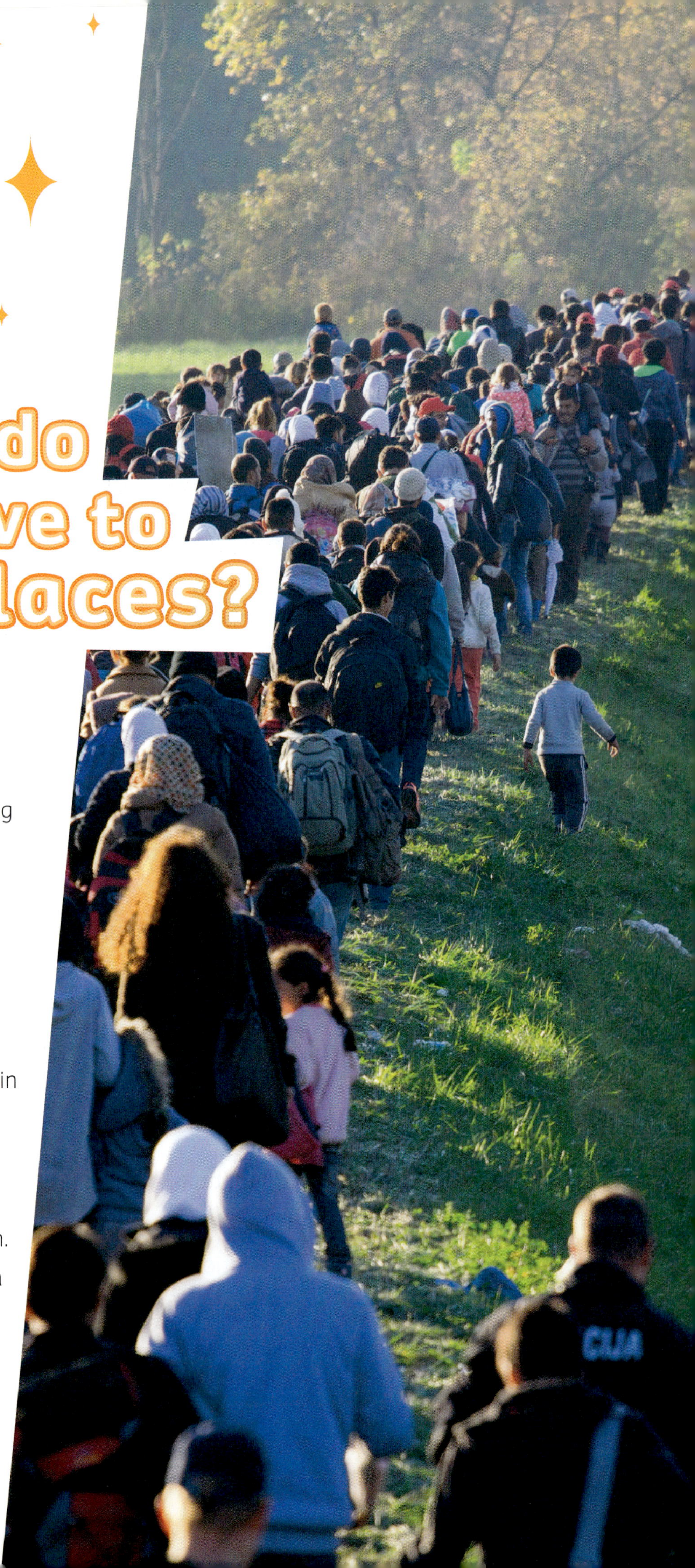

Listening
- I can recognize the relationship between a main point and supporting examples.
- I can identify the main points of factual talks.

Reading
- I can identify supporting details.
- I can understand details in longer texts.

Speaking
- I can give reasons for a choice or course of action.
- I can give an opinion in a structured discussion.

Writing
- I can write descriptions of personal experiences.

1 Look at the picture and discuss.

1 What are the people doing?
2 What are they carrying? Why?
3 How are the children the same as you? How are they different?

2 Read and make notes. Then compare your answers with a friend.

1 Do you know anyone who moved to a different country?
2 What did they like about it?
3 What do you think people miss when they move to a new country?

3 3-1 BBC Look at the video still and predict. Why are the girls packing a suitcase?

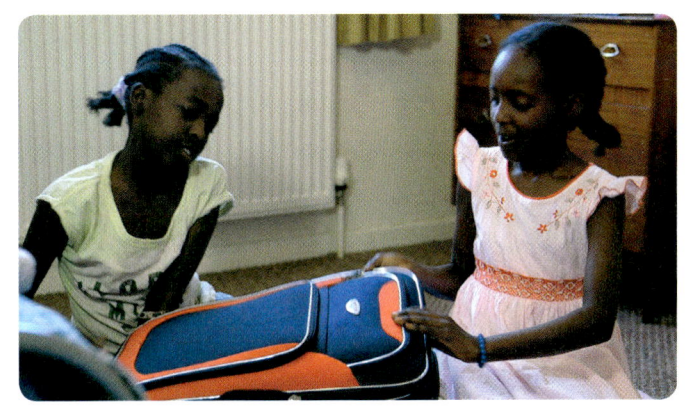

4 3-1 BBC Watch the video and check your answer from Activity 3. Then watch again and answer the questions.

1 Why did Rania and Marwa leave Sudan?

....

2 What do they think are the biggest differences between Sudan/Egypt and the U.K.?

....

3 How do the girls react to rain and snow?

....

37

Pre-reading 1

1 💬 Interview a friend about when they moved house or went to stay somewhere different.

1. Write three questions to ask them about the experience.
2. Ask and then answer with a friend.
3. Did you ask each other similar questions?

> 📖 **Reading strategy**
>
> Identify the causes of an event in a factual text.

2 💡 Read. What questions do you think Isabel was asked? Underline examples from the text to support your answers.

> Hi, I'm Agnes. I'm from Denmark, but I moved to Mexico with my mom, dad, and little sister when I was nine. We moved to Mexico because of my mom's work. My parents really wanted the opportunity for me and my sister to learn a different language as well. They thought we would benefit from all the different experiences. I was really nervous at first. I didn't speak very much on my first day at school! Now, a year later, I'm in Grade 5 and I love it!

3 🎧 1-15 Read *Moving On*. It's an article written from interviews with children. Did all of them move countries for the same reason?

Reading 1

MOVING ON
Interviews with young immigrants

Yulia, 10

I'm an **immigrant** to the United States.

I was born in Nickolaev, Ukraine, but now I live in a town in the state of New Jersey, which borders New York. I moved to the United States with my parents when I was six. I am now in the fourth grade and speak both English and Ukranian. Our **economic** and **political** situation wasn't good in Ukraine, so my father got a green card and got a job here.

I feel **settled** here in the United States. I **joined** a lot of clubs when I came here and have a lot of friends. Some of my favorite places to go are the ice-skating rink and the gymnasium. The thing I miss most about Ukraine is my grandmother, but we speak every week on Skype. I'd love her to come here, but she doesn't want to **move abroad**.

I'm from Mexico. Three years ago, I moved to Austin, Texas, to learn English. I didn't know any English when I got here. My mother, sister, brother, and I packed our baggage and belongings into our car and drove from our ranch in Coahuila to our new apartment in Austin. It's not far from the United States **border**, so the journey only took a day. My dad stayed behind on the **ranch**.

Leaving the ranch in Mexico was the hardest part about the move. I miss my two horses, my dog, and of course my dad! I was worried, but also excited to move. I didn't know anyone. I was really scared at first. My hardest moment was when I started school. At first, homework was really hard because everything was in English, and I didn't understand.

I like a lot of things about America. I especially like my teachers. They're really nice here and very helpful. I like the stores and the mall. My favorite music is hip-hop and rock. I want to stay here and become a U.S. **citizen**.

I talk with my friends on my computer and my phone. I get to go home to see my family, my animals, and my friends every school break.

Sofía, 14

Devante, 17

I was born in New Orleans, in the United States.

As an **environmental refugee**, I haven't moved countries, but I have moved to a different city hundreds of kilometers from my home. There was a huge **natural disaster** in my city – Hurricane Katrina – so we had to leave. I was only four when the hurricane hit, and I moved to Atlanta, which is another city in the United States, with my mom and two sisters. Leaving was chaotic. All I can remember was the wind and rain and water flowing like a river down our street. The floods after Katrina destroyed our home and all of our friends' and neighbors' homes. We went to Atlanta because my mother has a brother there, but all my friends were in different places.

In Atlanta, my sisters and I went to a new school. I missed my friends from New Orleans and I still don't know where some of them are, but I quickly made new friends. I'm in my final year of school now, and I want to be a meteorologist and study natural disasters such as hurricanes.

4 What do you think would be the hardest thing about moving to a new place? Why?

Comprehension 1

1 Read *Moving On* again. Why did they have to move?

1 Yulia: ....
2 Sofía: ....
3 Devante: ....

2 Read and write *Y* (Yulia), *S* (Sofía), and/or *D* (Devante).

1 Who had to learn a new language?
....
2 Whose home was destroyed?
....
3 Who still visits the place they came from?
....
4 Who do you think likes shopping?
....
5 Who do you think likes ice-skating?
....

3 Make inferences from *Moving On*. Work in groups of three.

1 **Student A:** write the questions you think the interviewer asked Yulia.
Student B: write the questions you think the interviewer asked Sofía.
Student C: write the questions you think the interviewer asked Devante.

2 Compare the questions you wrote with your group and with the class.

Listening 1

4 How would you feel if you had to move to a new country? Discuss with a friend.

Listening strategy
Distinguish between main information and extra details in answers.

5 (1-16) Listen. Whose mom from *Moving On* is speaking?

6 (1-17) Listen again. What information directly answers the questions and what's the extra detail? Write.

1 Why did you and your family migrate to the United States?
Direct answer: ....
Extra detail: ....

2 Did you speak any English before you arrived?
Direct answer: ....
Extra detail: ....

3 What do you miss about your home country?
Direct answer: ....
Extra detail: ....

40

Vocabulary 1

1 Find these words in *Moving On*. Then write them next to their definitions.

- border
- citizen
- economic
- environmental
- immigrant
- join
- move abroad
- natural disaster
- political
- ranch
- refugee
- settled

1 a large farm ....
2 related to money and the economy ....
3 someone who moved from another country ....
4 become part of a group/club ....
5 related to politics ....
6 a person who lives in a particular country ....
7 someone who needs to leave their country or region because it's dangerous to stay ....
8 related to the environment ....
9 feeling that you are at home ....
10 a line separating countries ....
11 change the country where you live ....
12 natural event which causes damage ....

2 🎧 Listen and say.
1-18

3 The word *border* is a noun and a verb. Find and circle both uses in *Moving On*. Which of these other words are both nouns and verbs? Can you add any more to the list?

| car | cut | door | dress | game |
| hand | milk | play | smell | tree |

4 💬 Play *Word Association* with a friend.

1 Start each time with a word from this lesson.
2 Take turns saying a word you associate with the previous word (all the words don't have to be from this lesson).
3 Continue until one of you pauses or repeats a word.

border,

Grammar 1

1 Watch Part 1 of the story video. Read and complete.

1 This evening, we're going to see _____ show.
2 We each have a map for _____ theater.

2 Look at the grammar box and read.

> **Grammar**
>
> **Articles**
>
> **Indefinite article: a/an**
> There's **an** elementary school and **a** junior high in my town.
>
> **Definite article: the**
> **The** bus of our school is yellow.
>
> **Zero article**
> My brother goes to school in Manila.

3 Read *Moving On* again. Circle the articles and their related nouns.

4 Read the rules for using articles and write *the*, *a/an*, or *0 (zero)*.

1. Use it when there's only one of something (including rivers, deserts, and superlative adjectives).
2. Use it to say what someone is or what job they do.
3. Use it when we have already mentioned the thing.
4. Use it with some places, e.g. school, home.
5. Use it with a singular noun to say something about all things of that kind.
6. Use it the first time you mention a single noun.
7. Use it before names, cities, and most countries.

5 Complete the sentences with *a/an* or *the*. If the sentence uses the zero article, don't write anything. Then number each sentence with the rules from Activity 4.

1 _____ Amazon river is _____ longest in the world. _____
2 _____ lion sleeps most of the day. _____
3 My mom's _____ immigrant to the United States. She's _____ paramedic. _____
4 My school is on _____ Cedar Road. I enjoy _____ school. _____
5 The teacher gave each group _____ map of the New York metro. _____ map she gave our group was really old. _____ _____

Speaking 1

6 Work with a friend. Prepare an interview with an immigrant to your country.

> **Speaking strategy**
>
> Try to read other people's body language. Are they feeling happy or uncomfortable?

7 Work with another friend. Take turns interviewing each other.

- **Interviewer:** Ask the questions you prepared; make the interview more spontaneous by asking questions you haven't prepared in response to answers given.
- **Interviewee:** Take the role of an immigrant to your country; give imaginative, realistic answers.

Prepared question	Answer	Spontaneous question
What made you move to this country?	Because this country needed workers with my skills and qualifications, and I wanted to travel.	Oh, really? So what skills and qualifications do you have?

Pre-reading 2

1 Think about your perfect way to spend a day. Discuss with a friend.

1 Describe where you are.
2 Talk about who you are with and what happens.

Reading strategy

Make inferences from details provided in a text.

2 Read. Who's the main character? Where is she?

They called it the motherland, but the only mother I wanted was the one I'd left behind in Trinidad. And there was no land to be seen in London, only grey buildings matching the grey skies. After only a few weeks in London, I could hardly believe that the huge blue Caribbean sky even existed. I was always cold. Even in August I was cold!

I'm Dominique Joseph and this was 1950s London. Britain needed us: welcomed us, in fact. They'd called out for nurses like me and workers to help their economy. Some of my friends and I answered Britain's call. We worked hard and made our home in Britain. We had a job to do, and we did it!

3 Read *Big Apple, Small World*. What are the different settings in the story? Who is the main character?

Reading 2

BIG APPLE, SMALL WORLD

Margaret ran out of the **wake** with tears pouring down her cheeks. She headed straight for her favourite place, the beach. She gazed out across the sea all the way to America. It seemed so, so far away. And so different from the little Galway town of Inverin where she'd grown up. That made her cry all over again. She was startled when a woman asked her, "Whose funeral is it?"

"Mine!" sobbed Margaret.

She told the **stranger** that she had run from her own wake.

"Well," said the woman, "you don't look dead to me. In fact, it looks like you've got your whole life ahead of you."

Margaret explained it was her American Wake. Most of her friends and family members were gathered at her home today. She would probably never see them again because, in two short days, she was setting sail for a new life in America where she would have to **integrate** into a new **society**. "I don't know when I'll see my family again!" she said.

44

"My son went to America last year," the woman said sadly. "There's nothing for young folk here. No work, no money, no future. We miss him, but he's happy there. If you want a friendly Galway lad to chat to when you're there, look up my son. His name's Patrick …" At that moment a huge wave crashed over Margaret and the kind woman, soaking them from head to toe.

"Oh," said Margaret, "I must go. My mum will think I jumped in the water," she added, looking at her wet clothes and laughing.

Two days later, Margaret was waving frantically at her family from the deck of the ship that was carrying her to New York. She stood there waving long after her family was out of sight, her sadness **increasing**. Margaret was 18 years old, had a one-way ticket to New York and only 25 cents in her pocket. Her only **luggage** was a small suitcase holding all her **belongings**.

Like most immigrants, Margaret **reunited** with family when she got to America. Her older sister, Mary, was waiting for her outside Ellis Island Immigration Station. Mary's friendly, familiar face was a welcome sight for the weary Margaret. As was the pleasant face of the Statue of Liberty rising above her. She felt a rush of excitement – she'd finally arrived!

Finding **employment** was **essential** and Margaret was working hard from day one. She washed floors on her hands and knees, she cooked, and she cared for other people's children. Her family in Ireland **benefited** from her wages because she sent a large part home.

One day Margaret was walking between jobs, looking in awe at the skyscrapers growing up around her. Suddenly she fell. Her shoe had completely **fallen apart**. She hopped and limped, carrying her shoe, to a nearby cobbler's stand.

She handed her shoe to the man at the stand. "It's been falling apart since it got soaked by a wave back in Ireland before I left," laughed Margaret.

"Was that on Inverin beach?" asked the young man, in a Galway accent. Margaret was shocked. She didn't know how he knew that. Then she remembered the woman on the beach. This was her son, Patrick! He knew all about the meeting from his mother's long letters to America. "My mother mentioned a girl," he said, "but I never thought I'd ever find you!"

Margaret and Patrick got married soon after and the rest, as they say, is history! Or, at least, my family history; for they were my grandparents all the way from Ireland. We still have family out there. In fact, we're having a family reunion in Inverin next month!

4 Do you think Margaret's story is different to migrant experiences today? How does it differ from the stories in *Moving On*?

Comprehension 2

1 💬 **Read the first half of *Big Apple, Small World*. Think about the settings.**

- Close your eyes and think about the setting at the beginning of the story.
- Share your ideas with a friend. What details in the text helped you imagine the setting?

2 **Read *Big Apple, Small World* again. Circle T (true) or F (false).**

1. Margaret ran away from her own wake. — T F
2. Margaret knew the woman on the beach. — T F
3. Margaret's sister was already in New York. — T F
4. Margaret had one job. — T F

3 **Complete the information about the characters. Circle the passages in the text that support your answers.**

Margaret

What I know about her
....

What I can guess about her
....

Patrick

What I know about him
....

What I can guess about him
....

4 💬 **Compare and discuss your answers from Activity 3. Then role-play a scene as Margaret and Patrick.**

Listening 2

5 💬 **Why do you think people traveled so far to get to America? Discuss with a friend.**

🎧 Listening strategy

Listen for key factual information, such as dates, numbers, and quantities.

6 🎧 1-20 **Listen. Which setting from *Big Apple, Small World* is the listening about?**

7 🎧 1-21 **Listen again and answer.**

1. How many immigrants passed through Ellis Island from 1892 to 1924?
   ....
2. Who was the first immigrant to come through Ellis Island?
   ....
3. How long were the inspections?
   ....

8 💬 **Discuss why Ellis Island was nicknamed both *Island of Hope* and *Island of Tears*.**

Vocabulary 2

1 Find these words in *Big Apple, Small World*. Then match the words to their definitions.

1 baggage (n)
2 belongings (n)
3 benefit (v)
4 employment (n)
5 essential (adj)
6 fall apart (v)
7 increase (v)
8 integrate (v)
9 reunite (v)
10 society (n)
11 stranger (n)
12 wake (n)

a when friends and family get together after someone dies
b a body of individuals living as members of a community
c to have or use something to your advantage
d to get together again after a separation
e someone you have never met before
f the suitcases you travel with
g to become part of a community
h something that's necessary
i to break into pieces
j to go up in number
k a job/occupation
l possessions

2 🎧 1-22 Listen, check your answers, and say.

🇬🇧 British	🇺🇸 American
luggage	baggage

3 Use the prefixes to write opposites.

anti   de   in   non   un

1 essential → *inessential*
2 increase → ....
3 employment → ....
4 integrated → ....
5 social → ....

4 💬 Complete the word clouds with words you associate with them. Compare with a friend.

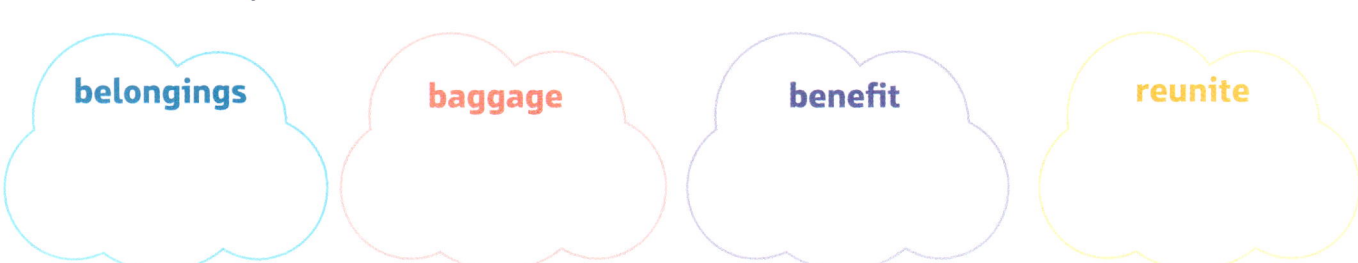

belongings   baggage   benefit   reunite

47

Grammar 2

1 🎬 3-1 BBC Watch Part 1 of the story video. Which word completes these three sentences? Read and complete.

1 I don't know _____ it is.
2 I know _____ the theater is.
3 Did you see _____ I put my red trainers?

2 Look at the grammar box and read.

> **Grammar**
>
> **Sentences containing question words**
> **Where** is a question word that is used in a sentence in Activity 1.
>
> **Who**, **which**, **when**, **what**, **why**, and **how (much/many/old)** can all be used in similar sentences with expressions like:
> I (can't) believe … , I (don't) know … , I (don't) see …

3 Read *Big Apple, Small World* again. Circle sentences with *wh-* words that are used outside of questions.

4 Read and complete.

> where   who   what   when   why   how

1 I don't see _____ we can resolve this problem.
2 I can't believe _____ he said.
3 Can you believe _____ they went on vacation?
4 She doesn't know _____ gave her the gift.
5 I don't see _____ they would do such a thing.
6 I really don't know _____ that happened.

48

5 Write the words in order.

1 didn't / I / where / see / went / she

....

2 the / left / do / why / know / they / you / movie theater

.... ?

3 moved / he / I / abroad / when / couldn't / it / believe

....

4 how / candy / see / I / didn't / took / they / much

....

5 she / to / who / talking / was / could / believe / you

.... ?

6 went / they / I / way / know / which / don't

....

6 Make a spinner. Play the game in pairs.

1 Make a six-sided spinner.
2 Write one of the question words on each side.
3 Start questions with *Do you know ...* then spin the spinner and complete the question with the word you get plus your own ideas.
4 Answer each other's questions.

7 Watch Part 2 of the story video. Who got lost?

Speaking 2

8 Work in groups. Discuss how you would create a tour of your town.

Group A: discuss how to create a tour for a student from a different country.

Group B: discuss how to create a tour for a student who is sight or hearing impaired.

Compare your ideas with other groups.

Writing

1 Scan the personal narrative. Answer the questions.

1 Which person from this unit wrote this narrative?

....

2 How do you think she felt on her first day at a new school?

....

2 Read and check your answers from Activity 1.

My First Day

I walked into a class full of strangers for the first time and wanted to be invisible. That's how I felt on my first day at school in Mexico. The teacher was telling the rest of the class all about me, but I didn't understand much of what she was saying. I spoke very little Spanish, so I only understood when she said my name and age. Some of the children smiled and waved, but others looked at me and whispered to each other. After what seemed like hours, I took my seat. That's when a girl leaned over and said, "Hola, soy Ines." I smiled at her and tried to remember what my Spanish teacher taught me, and after a moment's pause I said, "Hola, soy Isabel. ¿Qué tal?" Ines smiled. That was my first conversation in Spanish. Ines and I are still friends a year later, and I'll never forget her kindness that first day.

3 Read the narrative again. Answer the questions.

1 Which verb comes before the direct speech in the narrative?

....

2 Which other verbs can we use with direct speech?

....

Writing strategy

Use quotation marks to show direct speech in a text.
"Hello!" she said.

4 **WB 43** Think about the first time you did something. Then go to the Workbook to do the writing activity.

Now I Know

1 Why do we move to new places? Look back through Unit 3, remember what you learned, and write.

....
....
....

2 Choose a project.

Create a welcome message to an immigrant to your city.

1 Work in groups and look at your ideas for p49 Activity 8.
2 Decide on the media to deliver your welcome message.
3 Create your welcome message on your chosen media.

or

Research immigration to your country.

1 Find out about the immigrants who come to your country.
2 Record your findings using different charts and graphs.
3 Present the results of your research to the class.

Self-assessment

Check (✔) or cross (✘) for you.

✘ I can't do this yet.   ✔ I can do this.   ✔✔ I liked doing this.

I can recognize the relationship between a main point and supporting examples.
I can identify the main points of factual talks.
I can identify supporting details.
I can understand details in longer texts.
I can give reasons for a choice or course of action.
I can give an opinion in a structured discussion.
I can write descriptions of personal experiences.

4

How do we stay safe?

Listening
- I can understand details in extended dialogs.
- I can identify the main points of factual talks.

Reading
- I can identify problem/solution relationships.
- I can identify supporting details.

Speaking
- I can describe past events, using descriptive language to add interest.

Writing
- I can signal the sequence of actions or events.

1 💬 **Look at the picture and discuss.**

1 What do you think is happening?
2 What do you think the man is carrying? Why?
3 Do you think the people in the picture do an important job? Why? / Why not?

2 💬 **Read and make notes. Then compare your answers with a friend.**

1 How do your teachers and parents keep you safe?
2 Make a list of people whose job is to help us stay safe.
3 What can we do to keep ourselves safe?

3 ▶️ 4-1 BBC **Look at the video still and predict. How does this device keep us safe in the mountains?**

4 ▶️ 4-1 BBC **Watch the video and check your answer from Activity 3. Then watch again and answer the questions.**

1 What's the job of the Team Ski Patrol?
2 What's the first thing the Team Ski Patrol does every day?
3 Why are the flags so important?
4 How can a transceiver save a skier's life?
5 How long can a person survive under the snow?

Pre-reading 1

1 💬 Think about a time when you, or someone you know, had an accident. Discuss with a friend.

1. What happened?
2. Did someone help you (or the person you know)?
3. What did this person do?

> 📖 **Reading strategy**
>
> Identify problems and solutions described in the text.

2 💡 Read Chris's blog and answer. What's the problem? What's the solution?

| WHO WE ARE > | WHAT WE DO ⌄ | CAREERS ⌄ | SUPPORT US ⌄ |

My name's Chris. I'm a nurse with Doctors Without Borders, which is a medical charity that deals with emergencies all over the world. You have to prepare yourself to work in tough environments. I'm currently in Sierra Leone in Africa, helping people with a severe disease called Ebola. You also have to be attentive to people from different cultures. Yesterday, I saw a new mother. Her baby was very sick and in distress. But she refused to let me treat him because she had no money! When I told her that the treatment was free, she let me care for the child, who thankfully got better.

---

3 🎧 1-23 Read *Saving and Delivering Lives*. Why does Sophie like her job?

Reading 1

SAVING and DELIVERING LIVES

Sophie Williamson tells us all about her typical day as a paramedic.

My day begins at about 6:00 a.m. I arrive at work as some of my colleagues are going home. They work the night shift, and I work the day shift. The first call **happens** soon after I start work. We turn on the siren and drive quickly. There are normally three of us in an **ambulance**: the driver and two **paramedics**. We're a team, and we work well together. Teamwork is important when you're saving people's lives. We have different kinds of equipment on the ambulance. We have everything from a basic **first-aid kit** to treat minor **injuries** to a defibrillator for big emergencies, such as heart attacks.

On a busy day, we have about nine or ten incidents. A lot of these are accidents on the road or at home.

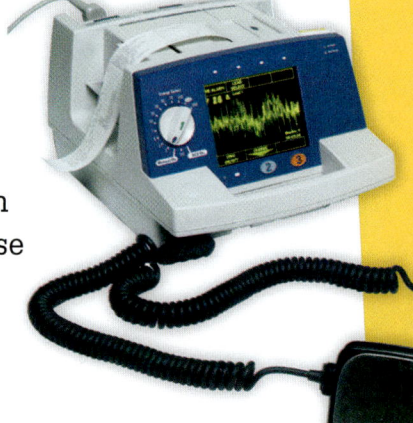

For example, an elderly person **falls over** and can't get back up, or a cyclist hurts herself in a collision with a car. If an injury is **severe**, we take the victim to the closest hospital. If they only have a minor injury, such as a swollen **ankle**, we treat them at the scene. Sometimes, we're called to a big emergency, and, when you first become a paramedic, it's important to prepare yourself for these stressful situations. I can remember my first call. It was a traffic accident on a highway involving 25 vehicles. There were about ten teams of paramedics on the scene, all treating the injured people. Some of these people were badly injured. They had to go to the hospital by air ambulance. Thankfully, they all survived.

I enjoy myself at work. It's a rewarding job. I love helping people and sometimes even saving their lives. I'm naturally a very attentive person, so being a paramedic is perfect for me. But it can be very tiring. Every day brings new challenges, and anything can happen! Take yesterday. One call sent me to a girl who had an accident while she was roasting marshmallows on a campfire. She fell over and **burned** herself quite badly on her left **elbow** and her left shoulder. The next call, however, was quite different. I was sent to attend to a pregnant woman. When we arrived at their apartment, her husband opened the door. His face was white, and he looked shocked. We **followed** him into the bedroom where his wife was **lying down** on the bed. She was in some distress. The baby was arriving, and I could see its head! We acted quickly, and we all helped to deliver the baby … even the husband. It was a girl, and the parents are going to call her Sophie after me. That's a great feeling!

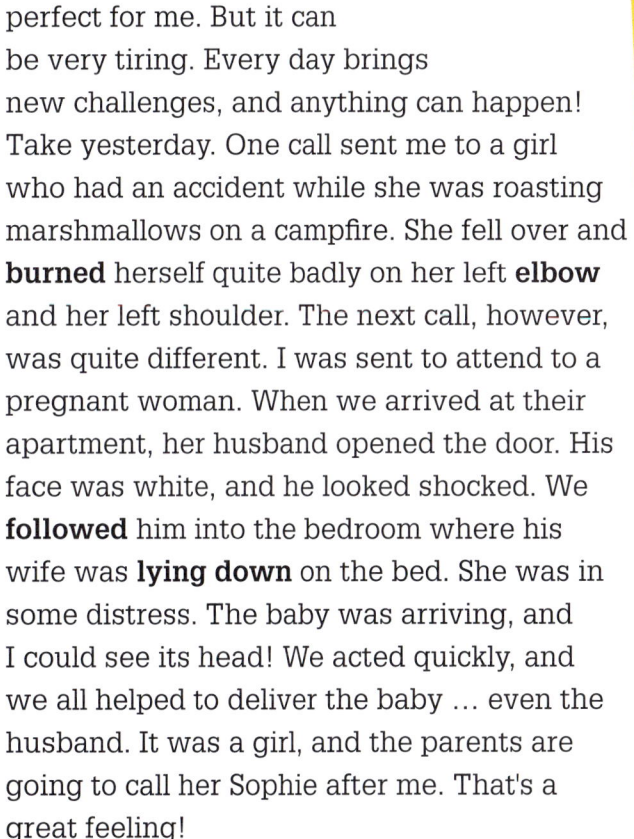

4 A paramedic is often the first person to arrive at the scene of an emergency. Do you think paramedics are more important than other first responders, such as doctors? Why / Why not?

Comprehension 1

1 Read *Saving and Delivering Lives* again. Find and write solutions to the problems.

1. Problem: a minor injury in a road accident
   Solution: ....
2. Problem: a major injury in a road accident
   Solution: ....
3. Problem: many injured in a big emergency
   Solution: ....

2 Correct the sentences.

1. Sophie can't remember her first big emergency.
   ....
2. The paramedics always take injured people to hospital.
   ....
3. Sophie doesn't think that teamwork is important when you're saving lives.
   ....
4. No paramedics work during the night.
   ....

Listening 1

> **Listening strategy**
> Focus on key information, such as dates, numbers, and quantities.

3 Look at the picture of an emergency. What can you see?

4 🎧 1-24 Listen to a TV news report about an emergency. What happened?

5 🎧 1-25 Listen again and answer.

1. How much rain fell in Georgemouth?
   ....
2. How many people had to be rescued?
   ....
3. At what time did it start to rain?
   ....
4. How long did the man wait before the National Guard rescued him?
   ....
5. When did the National Guard arrive in the town?
   ....

6 How do the emergency services help in emergency situations in your country? Discuss with a friend.

Vocabulary 1

1 Find these words in *Saving and Delivering Lives*. Then write them next to their definitions.

> ambulance　　ankle　　burn　　elbow　　fall over　　first-aid kit
> follow　　happen　　injury　　lie down　　paramedic　　severe

1 two parts of the body ....
2 something that contains items to treat minor injuries ....
3 a verb that means *to come after a person or thing* ....
4 an adjective that means *very bad* ....
5 a verb when fire hurts you ....
6 a verb that means *to take place* ....
7 a person who travels in an ambulance and treats you when you're injured or sick ....
8 a verb that means *to drop to the ground* ....
9 a verb that means *to be in a position in which your body is flat on a surface, such as a bed* ....
10 an emergency vehicle ....
11 damage to the body ....

2 Work in pairs. Ask and answer the questions.

1 When did you last fall over?
2 Have you ever burned yourself?
3 What injuries can happen at school?
4 Do you know what to do if someone gets hurt?

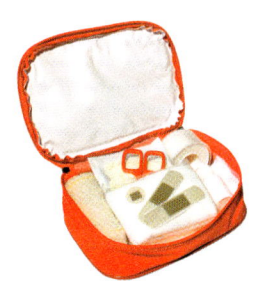

> I fell over at the skate park last Sunday and cut my knee. My mom put a Band-Aid on it.

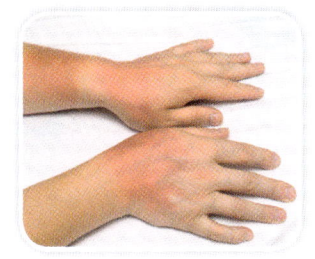

3 Watch Part 1 of the story video. What did Harry do?

4-2

57

Grammar 1

1 ▶ 4-3 BBC Watch Part 2 of the story video. What was Harry writing 1,000 times? Read and complete.

2 ▶ 4-3 BBC Watch Part 2 of the story video again. How did Harry hurt himself? What did Matilda do?

I should think of others, not only ....

3 Look at the grammar box and read.

Grammar

Reflexive pronouns

We use reflexive pronouns when the **subject** and the **object** of a sentence are **the same**.
She hurt **herself**.

4 Read *Saving and Delivering Lives* again. Circle the reflexive pronouns.

5 Complete the chart with the reflexive pronouns. Then complete the sentences below.

himself   itself   ourselves   themselves   yourself

I You He She It	burned	myself. .... herself.	We You They	burned	.... yourselves. ....

1 Jade's mom burned .... with hot water.
2 Tom didn't make .... a cup of coffee.
3 My mom and dad taught .... how to speak Spanish.
4 Have you ever hurt .... while you were at school?

6 Write sentences. Use the correct reflexive pronoun.

1 Emily / looks at / in the mirror before she leaves home.
Emily looks at herself in the mirror before she leaves home.

2 I / hurt / while I was playing soccer.
....

3 My dad / taught / to play the drums.
....

4 Watch out! / You're going to spill some coffee / and burn
....

5 We / dress / every morning before school.
....

6 They / always enjoy / when they go to the movies.
....

Speaking 1

7 Complete the profile with your own ideas.

All about me!

I hurt myself once when …
....

I really enjoy myself when …
....

because …
....

I taught myself to …
....

I learned how to dress myself when I was …
.... years old.

Speaking strategy

Make your story interesting by using adjectives for emotions.

8 Discuss your profile with a friend. Ask questions to get more information.

I taught myself to code. It made me feel great.

Cool! How did you learn?

Pre-reading 2

1 💬 What's a prank? Discuss with a friend.

1 Do you ever play pranks? If so, what kinds?
2 What kinds of prank are a bad idea?
3 How could a prank go wrong?

> 📖 **Reading strategy**
>
> Refer to details and examples when explaining what a text says explicitly.

2 Read. Why does Sophia want to become a firefighter? Circle the sentence that supports your answer.

> There was once a girl called Sophia who wanted to become a firefighter. Every night she dreamt of riding round the city in a big red fire engine, with the sirens sounding. She loved the excitement of racing to the scene of a fire and saving people's lives. The only problem was that Sophia was very scared of fire!

3 🎧 1-26 Read *The Boy Who Cried "Fire"*. How does Jack become a "lifesaver"?

Reading 2

THE BOY WHO CRIED FIRE

There was once a boy called Jack, who loved playing **pranks** all day long. For example, he would replace the sugar with some salt in the school dining hall. Can you imagine the look on the faces of the teachers after taking a sip of their morning coffee? But the prank Jack loved playing most of all was pretending that there was a fire. It could be at school, or it could be in the shopping centre. Wherever Jack was, he would find and set off the nearest **fire alarm**. He then loved seeing the **fire engines** arrive, quickly followed by the ambulances and the **police cars**. The only problem was that there never was a fire!

One warm summer day, Jack was sitting at his desk at school. "I don't want to be sitting here," he **complained** to himself. He started to daydream, imagining he was sunbathing on a tropical beach with a cold glass of juice in his hand and …

Ringaringaringaringaringaringaringaringaring!

The fire alarm **suddenly** sounded all through the school. Jack woke up from his daydream with everyone in the classroom looking at him.

"I didn't do anything!" he said innocently. He covered his ears and walked quickly outside with his class. The rest of the school **hurried** outside, too.

Before waiting long, **emergency** vehicles were outside. A firefighter jumped down from her fire engine and said immediately to Jack, "Is this one of your pranks again, Jack? We have been called out here four times already because of your practical jokes. You know our duty is to protect people and put out fires."

Jack quickly replied, "No. I'm not **lying**, and this isn't one of my pranks. I think there really is a fire this time. Look!"

He pointed up to a window on the second floor of the school building. There were yellow and orange flames that were **growing**, getting hotter and hotter.

"Where's that?" asked the firefighter. "It's the chemistry lab. Follow me," replied Jack.

Jack started to go into the school. "Wait," said the firefighter. "You can't go in there. It's not safe to go back into a burning building."

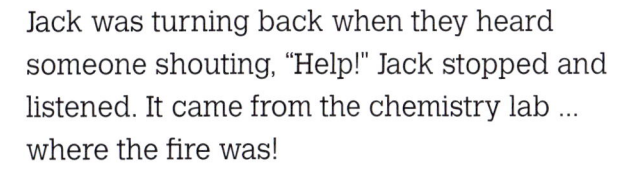

Jack was turning back when they heard someone shouting, "Help!" Jack stopped and listened. It came from the chemistry lab ... where the fire was!

"That's Mr Almeida, the science teacher! We have to go and help him!" shouted Jack.

"We'll go in," said the firefighter. "But we don't know where the chemistry lab is. Can you show us?"

Jack grabbed some chalk and drew a quick map on the ground. After looking at it, the firefighters ran into the building.

Smoke was everywhere, but the firefighters found the chemistry lab thanks to Jack's map.

"Thank you! You saved my life!" said Mr Almeida as they came out of the building.

The firefighters soon extinguished the flames, and the school was safe again. Jack's **heroic** actions saved the day.

"This time there really was a fire, Jack. You saved the school, and you saved Mr Almeida. You're a lifesaver," said one of the firefighters, as everyone cheered. "Let me give you some **advice**. Stop playing these pranks of yours, and one day you will become a firefighter too."

And from that day on, Jack never did play his favourite prank again.

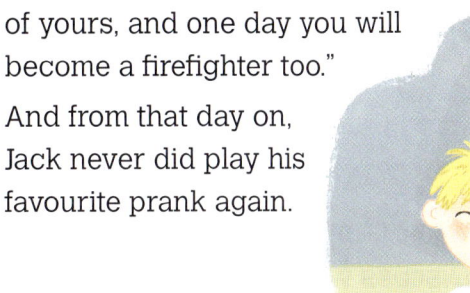

4 Firefighters don't only extinguish fires. What other emergencies do firefighters attend?

Comprehension 2

1 🗨 Read *The Boy Who Cried "Fire"* again. Why do you think the firefighter doesn't believe Jack at first? Discuss with a friend.

2 Number the events in order.

.... Jack pointed to the flames.
.... It was a nice day and Jack was at school.
.... Jack was bored, so he started to daydream.
.... The firefighters arrived.
.... Jack helped save Mr. Almeida.
.... The fire alarm went off.

3 Read and complete.

1 Jack loved to .... pranks.
2 His favorite prank was setting off fire ....
3 The .... soon arrived at the school.
4 Jack drew a .... of the building.
5 The firefighters rescued Mr. Almeida from the ....

Listening 2

4 🗨 What should you do in a fire drill? Discuss with a friend.

🎧 **Listening strategy**

Identify the main points of short, clear, factual talks or presentations on familiar topics.

5 🎧 1-27 Listen to the podcast about fire safety at school. What three things should every school do?

6 🎧 1-28 Listen again. Choose the best answers.

1 How many school fires are there every year in the United States?
  A There are 6,000 fires every year.
  B There are 60,000 fires every year.

2 What does every school need by law?
  A Every school needs their own firefighter by law.
  B Every school needs a fire alarm by law.

3 What's a fire drill?
  A It's a practice of the fire emergency procedures.
  B It's an instrument you use to put out a fire.

4 How often does a school have to do a fire drill?
  A A school has to do a fire drill every six months.
  B A school has to do a fire drill every month.

5 What does every room need?
  A Every room needs a map showing the emergency exits.
  B Every room needs a fire alarm.

7 🗨 What does your school do to protect you from fire? Discuss.

Vocabulary 2

🇬🇧 British	🇺🇸 American
fire engine	fire truck

1 Find these words in *The Boy Who Cried "Fire"*. Then complete the chart.

> advice   complain   emergency   fire alarm   fire truck   grow
> heroic   hurry   lie   police car   prank   suddenly

Nouns	Verbs	Adjectives
		Adverbs

2 🎧 1-29 Listen to the definitions. Write the words they refer to.

1 ....
2 ....
3 ....
4 ....
5 ....
6 ....
7 ....
8 ....
9 ....
10 ....
11 ....
12 ....

3 💬 Look at the pictures with a friend. What words from Activity 1 do you associate with each picture? Can you add any other words?

1
2
3

....
....
....

Grammar 2

1 🎬 4-2 BBC Watch Part 1 of the story video. What were they learning in class?

2 Look at the grammar box and read.

> ### Grammar
> The *-ing* form of the verb follows *after* and *before*.
> After **setting** off the fire alarm, Harry was in trouble.
> Before **setting** off the fire alarm, Harry was bored.

3 Read *The Boy Who Cried "Fire"* again. Circle the sentences with *after* or *before + -ing*.

4 Read and match.

1 After falling over the bag,
2 Before taking the man to hospital,
3 After putting out the fire,
4 Jane felt better
5 James read his book
6 Before cutting his finger with a knife,

a the firefighters left.
b before going to sleep.
c Marta hurt her leg.
d Michael was talking on the phone.
e the paramedics gave him some first aid.
f after taking the medicine.

5 Look and write sentences. Use *after* or *before + -ing*.

1 swim / Michael / walk to the beach

2 finish school late / Jane / run home

64

6 Complete the sentences. Write what you did yesterday.

1 Before going to school, ...
2 Before eating lunch, ...
3 After doing my homework, ...
4 After brushing my teeth, ...

Speaking 2

7 Read Ollie's list of activities last Saturday. Write sentences about what he did using *after* and *before* + *-ing*.

What I did last Saturday

1 Woke up early
2 Played tennis in the morning
3 Met friends in the afternoon
4 Ate pizza
5 Went home
6 Watched TV all evening

1 ....
2 ....
3 ....
4 ....
5 ....
6 ....

8 Write a list of all the activities you did last Saturday.

9 Work with a friend. Ask and answer questions about what you did.

What did you do on Saturday?

I ate breakfast before taking a shower.

Writing

1 Scan the poster about fire drills in a school. Answer the questions.

1 What do you do when you hear the fire alarm?
2 What do you do when you hear the all clear?

2 Read and check your answers from Activity 1.

What to Do in a Fire Drill

When you hear the fire alarm, get up from your chair and walk calmly from your classroom. Don't run and don't panic!

Then follow your teacher outside to the meeting point.

Next, wait with your class. Don't talk, and listen for any advice.

Before going back inside, listen for the all clear.

Finally, follow your teacher back to your classroom.

3 Read the poster again. Circle all the words that show a sequence of events.

4 Think about the fire drill procedures in your school. Then go to the Workbook to do the writing activity.

Writing strategy

Use a variety of transitional words and phrases to describe the sequence of events.
Then follow your teacher. **Finally**, go back to class.

66

Now I Know

1 How do we stay safe? Look back through Unit 4, remember what you learned, and write.

1 How can we keep ourselves safe?

....

....

2 Think about the jobs of a paramedic and a firefighter. How do they keep us safe?

....

2 Choose a project.

Research another "lifesaver" job.

1 Use books and the internet to research your chosen job.
2 Think about what this person does. Write and find pictures to create a presentation.
3 Present your research to the class.

or

Create a school safety brochure.

1 Think of all the things you can do to be safe at school.
2 Plan and design your brochure.
3 Write your brochure.
4 Present your brochure to the class.

Self-assessment

Check (✔) or cross (✘) for you.

✘ I can't do this yet.   ✔ I can do this.   ✔✔ I liked doing this.

I can understand details in extended dialogs.

I can identify the main points of factual talks.

I can identify problem/solution relationships.

I can identify supporting details.

I can describe past events, using descriptive language to add interest.

I can signal the sequence of actions or events.

5

Why do we protect animals?

Listening
- I can identify the main points of factual talks.
- I can recognize linking words/phrases signaling a sequence.

Reading
- I can scan texts to find specific information.
- I can guess the meaning of words from the context.

Speaking
- I can talk about past events or experiences.
- I can describe a funny or exciting personal experience.

Writing
- I can write letters with paragraph breaks.

1 💬 **Look at the picture and discuss.**

1. What kind of habitat does this animal usually live in?
2. Why do you think this animal may be endangered?

2 💬 **Read and make notes. Then compare your answers with a friend.**

1. How do we know an animal is endangered?
2. How do animals become extinct?
3. How can we protect endangered animals?

3 ▶ 5-1 BBC **Look at the video still and predict. Why does this animal need protection?**

4 ▶ 5-1 BBC **Watch the video and check your answer from Activity 3. Then watch again and complete.**

1. The sea otter is the .... marine mammal.
2. Otters were hunted to the brink of extinction in the 1700s and ....
3. One of the best places in the world to see otters is ....
4. Otters regularly use .... to get at their food.

69

Pre-reading 1

1 💬 Discuss with a friend.

1. Would you like any animal from the past to still be alive?
2. Which habitat would it live in?
3. Do you think it would need protection?

> **Reading strategy**
>
> Interpret information presented quantitatively.

2 Read about the IUCN Red List. How are species divided?

The IUCN (International Union for Conservation of Nature) Red List has information about the number of animals or plants that exist in a species. Based on this, each species is placed in a category, and this information helps us to decide which species need protection. The document contains other information, such as what experts are doing to help save the species, why the species is in danger and where it lives.

3 🎧 1-30 Read *Endangered Animals*. Which animals are critically endangered according to the IUCN Red List?

Reading 1

ENDANGERED ANIMALS

CAUSE

Experts believe that half of all animals will be extinct in the next 80 years and we'll only see many species in zoos. They agree this is because of the actions of humans. Humans have destroyed animals' habitats, hunted them and used some species in medicine. Climate change is another **threat** to animals as their habitats are destroyed by extreme weather, for example melting snow caps. In recent years, experts and governments have worked to protect many endangered species and their **environments** from disappearing.

AFRICAN WILD DOG

Status: EN
Population: 3,000
Threats: hunting, destruction of habitat
Conservation: kept in **captivity**

The biggest populations of the **African wild dog** are found in Botswana and Tanzania. However, this animal has become extinct from many other countries in Africa. It lives in forests, grasslands and deserts. The African wild dog eats other animals such as zebras and ostriches.

70

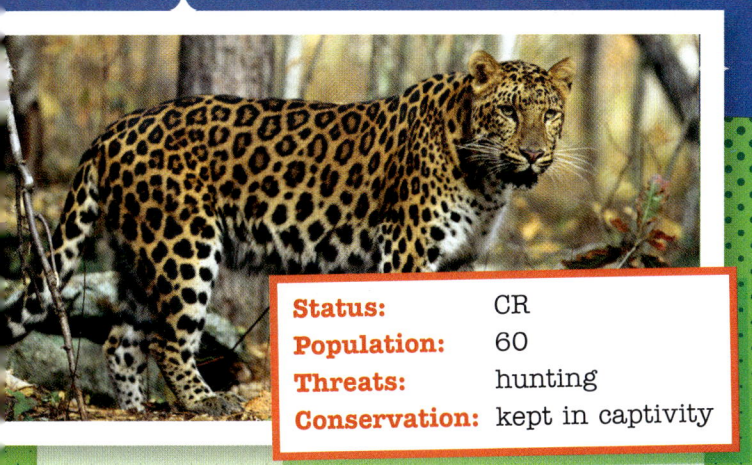

Status: CR
Population: 60
Threats: hunting
Conservation: kept in captivity

Amur Leopard

The **Amur leopard** lives in forests in Russia and China. It's the most endangered cat species in the world. It's been **missing** from Korea since 1969. There aren't many examples of this animal in the wild and an estimated 180 are kept in zoos. Experts want to **release** the Amur leopard back into its natural habitat. This animal normally eats other **mammals** such as deer and rabbits.

Status: CR
Population: between 220 and 275
Threats: hunting, destruction of habitat
Conservation: sanctuaries in Indonesia, kept in captivity

Sumatran Rhino

This is the smallest member of the rhino family. It's found on the islands of Sumatra and Borneo in Asia. The **Sumatran rhino** lives in **tropical** rainforests in the mountains. In the past, you could find it in many countries throughout the continent. Like all rhinos, this species only eats the leaves of trees and plants.

Status: CR (Asia); EN (Africa)
Population: unknown, but is expected to decrease by 90% in the coming years
Threats: hunting
Conservation: **sanctuaries** in many countries, patrols to prevent hunting

IUCN Red List Categories

EX – Extinct. No known individuals remaining.
EW – Extinct in the wild. Only survives in captivity.
CR – Critically endangered. Extremely high risk of extinction.
EN – Endangered. High risk of extinction.
VU – Vulnerable. High risk of endangerment in the wild.
NT – Near threatened. Likely to become endangered in the wild.
LC – Least concern. No danger for this species.

Pangolin

The **pangolin** is small with a very long tail. It's got scales all over its body to protect it from its predators such as lions, tigers, and leopards. When it's under threat, the pangolin rolls up into a ball and its scales become like a shield. The pangolin lives in the rainforests and grasslands of Africa and Asia. It eats insects such as ants and beetles. In Asia, the pangolin has become critically endangered. Experts believe the animal will soon be extinct.

4 Why do people hunt animals? Can hunting an animal ever be justified? Give reasons.

Comprehension 1

1 Read *Endangered Animals* again and answer.

1 Are there more Amur leopards or African wild dogs?

2 What percentage of all animals are likely to be extinct within 80 years?

2 Read the fact files again and answer the questions.

1 Why is the African wild dog endangered?

....

....

2 Which animals do experts keep in captivity?

....

....

3 Which animal can we find in two different continents?

....

4 Which animals are in danger because people destroy their habitat?

....

....

3 Read and complete.

1 Both the .... and the .... live in rainforests.

2 The .... is the only animal to live in the desert.

3 The .... is the only animal not to eat meat.

4 Experts believe the .... will soon be extinct.

5 There are almost 200 .... in captivity.

72

Listening 1

4 Why do you think people have hunted the Amur tiger? Discuss with a friend.

Listening strategy

Predict facts on the basis of general knowledge.

5 2-01 Listen to the interview about the Amur tiger. Why is it endangered?

6 2-02 Circle **T** (true) or **F** (false). Then listen again to check.

1 In the past there were only 40 Amur tigers in existence.   T F

2 China was the first country in the world to protect the tiger.   T F

3 The Amur leopard and the Amur tiger live in different habitats.   T F

7 In what ways can governments help endangered species? Discuss with a friend.

Vocabulary 1

1 Find these words in *Endangered Animals*. Then complete the chart.

> African wild dog   Amur leopard   captivity
> environment   mammal   missing   pangolin   release
> sanctuary   Sumatran rhino   threat   tropical

Adjectives	Nouns	Verbs

2 Read the extract from the text, then the two definitions of *environment*. Which definition is correct according to the extract?

> ... experts and governments have worked to protect many endangered species and their environments ...

environment *n*
1 the specific surroundings in which a person or an animal lives
2 the Natural World in general

3 Many words in English have more than one meaning, like *environment*. What words do you know in English that have more than one meaning?

4 💬 Discuss with a friend.

1 What other endangered animals do you know?
2 What threats do endangered animals face in the wild?
3 What are the positives and negatives of keeping animals in captivity?

Grammar 1

1 Watch Part 1 of the story video. What was Jade learning about today? Read and complete.

Jade .... a song about endangered animals.

2 Read the grammar box and circle.

3 Read *Endangered Animals* again. Circle the sentences with the Present Perfect.

Grammar

Present Perfect

I've **visited** the United States.   She **hasn't eaten** the pizza.   **Have** you **written** a book?
We can use *for* and *since* with **Present Perfect**. We use *for* when we want to talk about the duration of an activity. We use *since* when we want to talk about when an activity started.

1   He's lived here **since** / **for** 2012.
2   He's lived here **since** / **for** ten years.

4 Complete the chart with the time expressions from the box. Can you think of any more time expressions to add?

| 1998   a couple of hours   a week   five days   last week   many years
  May   she was 11   the start of the year   two minutes |

for

since

5 Read and complete. Use the Present Perfect form of the verb in parentheses and *for* or *since*.

Animals Return from Extinction

Experts want to introduce animals that ¹_____ (be) extinct from the U.K. ²_____ many years. There's a project to introduce the lynx, a member of the big cat family. People in the U.K. ³_____ (not see) this animal ⁴_____ the year 800. "We ⁵_____ (work) to return the Eurasian lynx to the U.K. ⁶_____ a long time," said Jane Donaldson, an animal expert. There are also plans to introduce the Eurasian beaver to Scotland. This animal ⁷_____ (be) extinct from the U.K. ⁸_____ 300 years.

Eurasian lynx

Eurasian beaver

6 Ask and answer with a friend. Give two answers for each question, using both *for* and *since*.

> How long has the Eurasian lynx been extinct from the U.K.?

> It's been extinct from the U.K. for about 1,200 years!

Speaking 1

7 Complete the sentences with information about you. Use *for* and *since*.

1 (live) in this town
I've lived in this town for five years.

2 (know) my best friend
_____

3 (be) in this class
_____

4 (be) interested in sports/music/art
_____

8 Ask and answer with a friend using *How long … ?* Use the information from Activity 7.

> How long have you lived in this town?

> I've lived here since 2017.

> That's a long time!

75

Pre-reading 2

1 💬 A pest is any small animal that destroys plants and food. Do you think all insects are pests? Discuss with a friend.

📖 **Reading strategy**

Determine the meaning of words and phrases in context.

2 💡 Read the text and find the words and expressions from the box. What do you think they mean? Do you have any similar expressions in your own language?

Herculean   nemesis   to open Pandora's box

Saving the planet's animals and plants was always going to be difficult. Very difficult. In fact, Herculean you could say. You see, humans thought that they could do whatever they wanted to do when it came to other living things. We hunted them, we destroyed their homes. They saw us as their ultimate nemesis. An enemy to be avoided. But the real problems began when humans started to destroy all the insects. That was when they opened Pandora's box.

3 🎧 2-03 Read *Pollinators and Pandora's Box*. Find and circle the words and expressions from Activity 2.

Reading 2

POLLINATORS AND PANDORA'S BOX

The planet Earth is now very different to what it was like in 2024. It's such a hot place to live and a lot of the lakes and rivers are now dry. There are no fish in the ocean and very few birds in the sky. Many of the animals you know and love have gone forever. There's no African elephant and certainly no giant tortoise. It's a tragedy this has happened, that the planet has gone from being a place with a lot of wildlife to what it is today: barren and inhospitable. **Ecosystems** like rainforests, grasslands, and rivers are **rare** or don't exist anymore.

Maria doesn't go to school. No child does. In fact, nobody leaves their home because the conditions outside are so dreadful. It's a Herculean effort to spend just a few minutes in the open air.

76

Instead, Maria has classes over the internet. Her favorite class is history. This is because she learns all about life just a few decades ago. And Mr. Socrates, the history professor, is her favorite teacher. He's such an old man he can remember all the extinct animals. He can also remember eating crunchy apples and juicy oranges … not the **flavorless** tablets we eat now.

"Tell me again what it was like when you were a boy, Mr. Socrates," Maria often asks.
"It was wonderful. It was when you could stop to smell a flower and climb a tree to pick a fresh apple."
"Why have trees stopped producing fruit and why have plants died?"
"The answer is very simple, Maria: pollination."
"What's that?"
"Pollination is when a certain type of insect, like a **bumblebee** or a butterfly, lands on a flower and takes the **pollen** to another flower. The second flower creates a **seed**. From this seed another flower grows."
"Do these insects help flowers to make more flowers?"
"That's right, Maria. We call these insects pollinators. Can you guess what happened when all the pollinators died?"
"Pollination stopped, and trees and plants stopped making new plants."
"Exactly! They also stopped producing fruit and vegetables for us to eat. It was such a shame when that happened."
"Why did the pollinators become extinct?"
"It was a number of things. They lost their natural habitats. As we made more buildings and roads, we destroyed their homes. Can you think of any more reasons, Maria?"

"Um … climate change?"
"Yes, that's right. The hotter summers and colder winters destroyed **entire** species of pollinators. But their biggest nemesis was pesticides. Do you know what these are?"
"Are they **chemicals** to protect crops from insects that want to eat them?"
"Correct! But farmers didn't understand they were opening Pandora's box with these chemicals. Pesticides killed the insects that wanted to eat the crops. They also destroyed the insects that didn't want to eat the crops, like the pollinators."
"Therefore, the loss of habitat, climate change, and the use of pesticides upset the **balance** of **nature**. Is that right, Mr. Socrates?"
"It is! The disappearance of pollinators then destroyed the **biodiversity** of many places around the world. Do you know why?"
"Because other animals, such as birds and small mammals, eat insects. Without this **source** of food, they started to disappear."
"Soon there were no insects, no birds, no flowers, no trees, and no food! We've taken these horrible tablets ever since."
"Is there anything that our ancestors could have done?"
"The answer, Maria, is yes. They could have …"

4 The story describes a future that could happen. What can we do now to try and make sure this doesn't happen?

Comprehension 2

1 Read *Pollinators and Pandora's Box* again. Match the characters to their descriptions.

1 Hercules ......
2 Pandora ......
3 Nemesis ......

a She was the first woman, and had a box containing many bad things.

b This was a very strong man who completed 12 very difficult tasks.

c This was a goddess who took vengeance on bad people.

2 Is the story set in the past, the present, or the future? Underline the sentences in the first paragraph that justify your answer.

3 What three reasons are mentioned for the extinction of pollinators? Discuss with a friend.

Listening 2

4 Work with a friend. Choose one paragraph each. Take turns reading your paragraph and explaining how insects help people.

1 Some cultures around the world use insects to treat people with injuries or disease. In China, people use insects to treat snakebites.

2 Insects can help us make money. Bees produce honey which stores sell and we buy. Silkworms produce silk that we use for clothes.

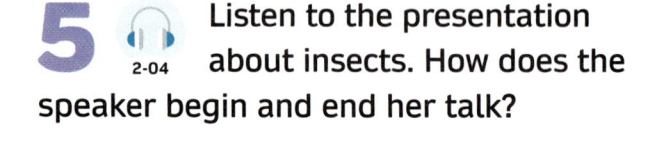

5 2-04 Listen to the presentation about insects. How does the speaker begin and end her talk?

6 2-05 Listen again and answer.

1 In the introduction, why does the speaker say that some people think that insects are pests?

2 According to the speaker, how have we used honey throughout history?

3 How did Chinese merchants use silk?

7 Why are insects so important? Should we make an extra effort to protect them? Discuss with a friend.

Listening strategy

Identify words and expressions that introduce and conclude a formal talk.

78

Vocabulary 2

1 Find these words in *Pollinators and Pandora's Box*. Then write them next to their definitions.

> balance   biodiversity   bumblebee
> chemicals   ecosystem   entire   flavorless
> nature   pollen   rare   seed   source

1. a powder that flowers produce
2. the environment, all the plants and animals connected with each other
3. with nothing left out, complete
4. many different kinds of living things
5. without any taste
6. everything in the world that people have not made
7. when different things are in the right amounts
8. the place that something comes from

2 Look at the words from Activity 1 that you didn't use. Explain their meaning to a friend.

3 Read and complete. Use the words from Activity 1.

There's a ¹_____ in the ²_____ when all plants, animals, and the environment are well connected with each other. There's a variety of living things and this ³_____ means that we can see common species, as well as ⁴_____ flowers and animals, safe in their natural environment. The ⁵_____ and the wind carry ⁶_____ from one flower to another and ⁷_____ meadows become covered in beautiful blossoms.

4 Rainforests, grasslands, and rivers are examples of ecosystems. Can you think of any more examples? Why do you think biodiversity is so important? Discuss with a friend.

Grammar 2

1 Watch Part 2 of the story video. How does Jade describe Mr. Perkins? Read and complete.

He's such a _____!

2 Look at the sentence in Activity 1. Circle the correct meaning.

1 Mr. Perkins is a person that lived a very long time ago.
2 Mr. Perkins is a person who is very old-fashioned.

3 Read the grammar box and answer.

> **Grammar**
>
> **so** and **such**
>
> **A**
> It's hot.
> It's a hot day.
>
> **B**
> It's **so** hot.
> It's **such** a hot day.
>
> 1 What kind of word follows **so**?
> 2 What kind of word follows **such**?

4 Read *Pollinators and Pandora's Box* again. Circle the sentences with *so* or *such*.

5 Read and circle.

1 This is **so** / **such** an interesting book!
2 My shower was **so** / **such** short this morning.
3 The art show was **so** / **such** great!
4 You wrote **so** / **such** an amazing song!
5 My dad was **so** / **such** angry when I came home late last night.
6 I never knew that she was **so** / **such** a popular artist.

80

6 Read and complete. Use *so* or *such a/an*.

1. I'm _____ tired.
2. James is _____ computer geek.
3. She's _____ thirsty.
4. These clothes are _____ old-fashioned.
5. Mexico City is _____ big place.

> *so* and *such* can often be used in sentences that mean the same.
>
> an interesting book   It's **such** an interesting book.
>   This book is **so** interesting.

7 Read and write sentences that mean the same. Use *so* or *such a/an*.

1. This bus ride is so long. *This is such a long bus ride.*
2. It's such a scary movie. _____
3. This building is so tall. _____

Speaking 2

Speaking strategy
Use intonation to express excitement.

8 What would you say in these situations? Write sentences with *so* or *such*.

1. It's early in the morning and you feel sleepy.

   _____

2. You notice that your friend has long hair.

   _____

3. It's dinnertime and you haven't eaten since midday.

   _____

9 Write five of your own situations. Then role-play with a friend.

> It's so exciting!
>
> Yes! It's such an amazing game!

Writing

1 Read the letter and answer.

1. What animal does Pedro want to save?
2. Why does he want to save it?

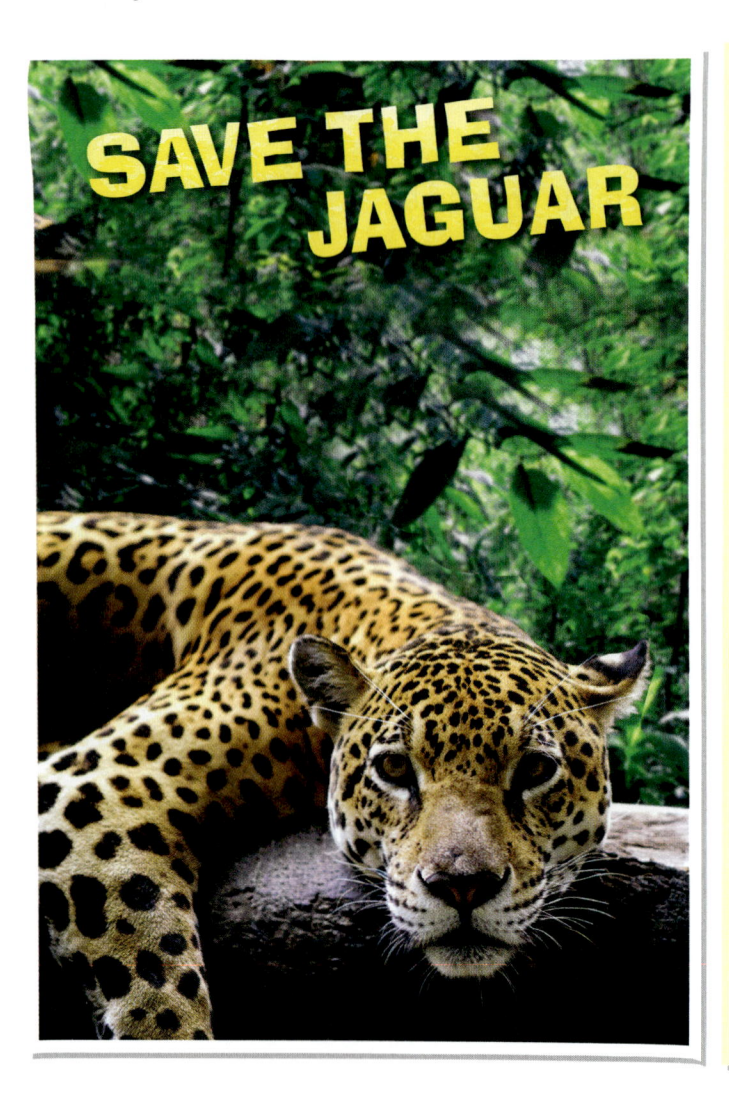

SAVE THE JAGUAR

Dear Sir/Madam,

I'm writing to ask you to pass a law to protect the jaguar. This animal will soon be extinct.

The jaguar is under threat because we're destroying its habitat to make new roads and new buildings.

The jaguar is important because it eats other animals, such as deer. This is important because deer eat some of the food that farmers grow for us.

Please introduce laws to save the jaguar.

Yours truly,
Pedro Jimenez de Santos

2 Read the letter again. Match the paragraphs to their descriptions.

1. Summary and conclusion
2. Reason for writing
3. Complimentary close and name
4. Main arguments
5. Greeting

Writing strategy

Divide a letter into clear paragraphs. Remember about the greeting, complimentary close, and signature.

3 WB 71 Find a picture of an animal you want to protect. Then go to the Workbook to do the writing activity.

82

Now I Know

1 Why do we protect animals? Look back through Unit 5, remember what you learned, and write.

We need to protect animals because different species help create biodiversity.

2 Choose a project.

Work in a group to create a campaign about endangered animals.

1 Think of endangered animals and gather information about them.
2 Plan and design your campaign. How are you going to tell your friends about endangered animals?
3 Create the material that you need.
4 Present and launch your campaign.

or

Create a fact file on an endangered animal.

1 Research your chosen animal.
2 Describe this animal, where it lives, why it's endangered, and what we can do to help it.
3 Write some notes and find pictures to create a fact file.
4 Present your fact file to the class.

Self-assessment

Check (✓) or cross (✗) for you.

✗ I can't do this yet.   ✓ I can do this.   ✓✓ I liked doing this.

I can identify the main points of factual talks.
I can recognize linking words/phrases signaling a sequence.
I can scan texts to find specific information.
I can guess the meaning of words from the context.
I can talk about past events or experiences.
I can describe a funny or exciting personal experience.
I can write letters with paragraph breaks.

6
What's literature?

Listening
- I can understand the main points of an interview.
- I can identify opinions.

Reading
- I can compare information in different texts on the same topic.
- I can make inferences about characters' motives and feelings.

Speaking
- I can give an opinion in a structured discussion.
- I can talk about matters of personal interest.

Writing
- I can write a review of a book.

1 Look at the picture and discuss.

1 What's this place?
2 Why did people build such places in the past?
3 Do we need such places now?

2 Read and make notes. Then compare your answers with a friend.

1 What kind of books do you like to read? Why?
2 Do you read books online?
3 Do you go to the library?

3 BBC Look at the video still and predict. Where are they? What are they talking about?

4 BBC Watch the video and check your answers from Activity 3. Then watch again and answer the questions.

1 What job does Rachel Denwood do?
   ....
2 How many books and manuscripts does she read every year? ....
3 What feedback do Jack and Megan get on their stories? Write one tip.
   ....
4 Why is the blurb important?
   ....

85

Pre-reading 1

1 💬 Discuss with a friend.

1. Do you read magazines?
2. Do you have a favorite magazine?
3. What do you read online?

> 📖 **Reading strategy**
>
> Describe how information is compared in a text.

2 💡 Read. How are newspapers and magazines similar and how are they different?

We read newspapers and magazines to get information. They both contain news about events around the world. Newspapers have short news stories with lots of facts. In magazines, however, news stories are longer. You can buy newspapers every day. You can buy magazines every week or every month. They both can contain articles about travel, fashion, or films.

3 🎧 2-06 Read *What Do You Feel Like Reading?*. What's the definition of literature according to most dictionaries?

Reading 1

What Do You Feel Like Reading?

Do you feel like reading a **novel**, a poem or a blog? And which of those is literature? Some people would say literature is "stories in books" and nothing else. Others will say that only **authors** such as William Shakespeare, Gabriel García Márquez, and Orhan Pamuk can write literature. Look in a dictionary, however, and the answer is different. Most dictionaries say that anything that's written is "literature". So, what you read in **newspapers** and magazines, **publish** on your blogs or even what you're reading now is literature. Let's look at some popular forms of literature.

Novels

A novel is a work of **fiction**. It's typically got a plot. The **plot** is the main story and it's often got the same structure: a beginning, a middle and an end. In the beginning of the plot, the story and the main characters are introduced. In the middle, the plot develops and sometimes there is conflict. At the end, the story concludes. Authors who are **popular** with young people include Michael Morpurgo and Suzanne Collins.

86

Short Stories

Want to read, but don't feel like reading a whole novel? A short story is like a novel, but shorter! On average, a novel contains about 120,000 words. A short story has got fewer words – between 1,000 and 20,000. Like a novel, a short story has got a plot and different **characters**. A short story has also got a beginning, a middle and an end. Many authors who write novels also write short stories.

Flash Fiction

If you think that a short story is, well, short, then how about flash fiction? Flash fiction often contains six words. Despite their length, many flash fiction stories have got a main character and a plot. People think this is a new kind of literature. This isn't true. People have written flash fiction for thousands of years.

Blogs

Blogging is a new kind of literature. It's become very popular over the past few years, especially with young people. More than 400 million people regularly read blogs. The **content** of blogs can range from news stories, similar to newspapers and magazines, to opinions about fashion, cinema or gaming. You can be a blogger if you've got the right equipment. You don't need a pen and paper. You need **innovative** technology such as a tablet or a smartphone. You can write whatever you feel like writing about!

Poetry

A poem describes places, things, people or feelings using beautiful, descriptive language. A poem can also tell a story. Poems use a lot of metaphors. A **metaphor** is an expression that doesn't quite mean what you first think it means. An example is "The peaceful lake was a mirror." Poems often rhyme. This means that a word at the end of one line sounds similar to a word at the end of a previous line. Poems can be structured into short verses. This is different from novels, which have got sentences and paragraphs.

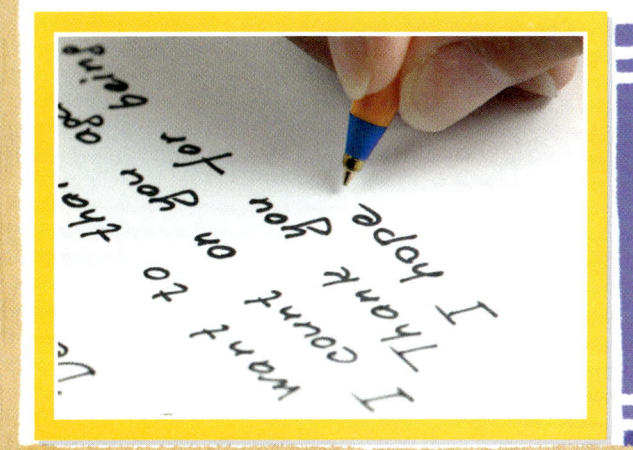

Personal Correspondence

Yes, you read right. Your emails, letters and even your WhatsApp messages are literature. OK, they may not have a plot, characters or metaphors, and the words may not rhyme, but every time you put pen to paper, or use text speak like CUL8R (see you later), you're following in the footsteps of Shakespeare!

4 Do you agree with the last paragraph? Do you think your text messages are literature?

Comprehension 1

1 Read *What Do You Feel Like Reading?* again and answer the questions.

1 How are novels and short stories similar?

....

2 How does poetry differ from novels?

....

3 How are blogs and letters similar?

....

4 How does flash fiction differ from short stories?

....

5 What kinds of content can be on a blog?

....

6 What kinds of literature have a plot?

....

2 Work in pairs and answer the questions. There may be more than one answer.

According to the text, which kind of literature …

1 tells you what's happened recently?
2 can you read very quickly?
3 sometimes contains personal opinions?
4 uses very descriptive language?
5 can be written by anyone?
6 is new?

3 What makes an author successful? Think and write.

....

....

Listening 1

4 Do you like writing? Have you ever written a story? Discuss with a friend.

Listening strategy

Understand the main points of a short, informal interview.

5 2-07 Listen to the interview with Vicky Jamieson, a successful young author. What's *fan fiction*?

6 2-08 Listen again. What advice does Vicky give? Check (✓) the correct answers.

People who want to become authors should …

1 read a lot of books. ☐
2 write fan fiction. ☐
3 rarely write. ☐
4 have a good idea what the plot is before starting. ☐
5 only sleep a little before writing. ☐

7 Many people read literature because they like stories. What other reasons are there? Discuss with a friend.

Vocabulary 1

1 Find these words in *What Do You Feel Like Reading?*. Write a definition for each one in your own words.

1. author (n)
2. character (n)
3. content (n)
4. fiction (n)
5. innovative (adj)
6. metaphor (n)
7. newspaper (n)
8. novel (n)
9. poetry (n)
10. plot (n)
11. popular (adj)
12. publish (v)

2 Look at Activity 1. How did you figure out the meaning of each word? Number the techniques you used.

1. I already knew the word.
2. It's similar to a word in my own language.
3. I used the context of the word.
4. I used a dictionary.

3 Work in pairs. Choose a kind of literature or a word from Activity 1. Take turns describing and guessing.

> This is a kind of literature that includes a story that someone has written.

> A novel!

4 Discuss with a friend.

1. Can you describe the plot of your favorite novel?
2. Can you name any popular authors in your country? What have they written?
3. Do you read poems? If so, can you recite any of your favorite poems?

5 Watch Part 1 of the story video. What was Jade's class about? What task did Mr. Fisher give them?

Grammar 1

1 Watch Part 2 of the story video. What does Jade want to do next? Read and complete.

I feel like ....

2 Watch Part 2 of the story video again. Why does Jade draw a cartoon?

3 Look at the grammar box and read.

> **Grammar**
>
> We use **feel like** + **verb** + **-ing** to talk about activities that we'd like to do at that moment.
>
> He **feels like writing** a blog. (At this moment in time he wants to write a blog.)
> I **don't feel like going** outside. (At this moment in time I want to stay inside.)

4 Read *What Do You Feel Like Reading?* again. Circle sentences with *feel like*.

5 Read and match.

1 The ocean looks nice and clear.
2 This subject is too difficult.
3 It's raining.
4 I'm hungry.
5 This party is boring.
6 This music is really cool.

a I feel like having a snack.
b I feel like dancing.
c I feel like going home.
d I feel like going for a swim.
e I don't feel like going out.
f I don't feel like studying.

6 Look and write. Use *feel like* or *don't feel like*.

1 I don't feel like watching TV.

2 ....

3 ....

4 ....

Speaking 1

7 Complete the chart. Check (✓) the activities you feel like doing.

What I feel like doing today	Yes
going for a walk	☐
writing a short story	☐
eating fast food	☐
eating fresh fruit	☐
messaging friends	☐
talking with my parents	☐
playing sports	☐

Speaking strategy

Refuse in a polite way. Use *sorry*.

8 Work in pairs. Tell a friend what you do and don't feel like doing today.

It's so sunny. I feel like going for a walk.

Me, too!

Do you want to play baseball?

I don't feel like playing sports today, sorry.

Pre-reading 2

1 💬 Discuss with a friend.

1. Is a diary a kind of literature?
2. Why do people keep diaries?
3. Do you know anyone who keeps a diary?

> 📖 **Reading strategy**
>
> Describe a character's feelings using details in a first-person narrative.

2 💡 Read Michael's diary. How do you think he's feeling? Why is he feeling this way?

March 18

It's been the best day ever! Mom and I have been alone at home for more than six months. Dad has been away because of his job. He's a scientist and he's been in a lot of different countries helping at new laboratories. But today was the day we've been waiting for – he finally came home. We were all so excited! Mom started crying, and so did Dad. But I didn't because I'm not a baby. He brought me a fantastic gift – a new video games console. How cool! You can't even buy it in this country yet! All my friends want to come to my house to play it.

3 🎧 2-09 Read *Eyes in the Dark*. How do you think Isabel is feeling on July 30? Circle the reasons for your answer.

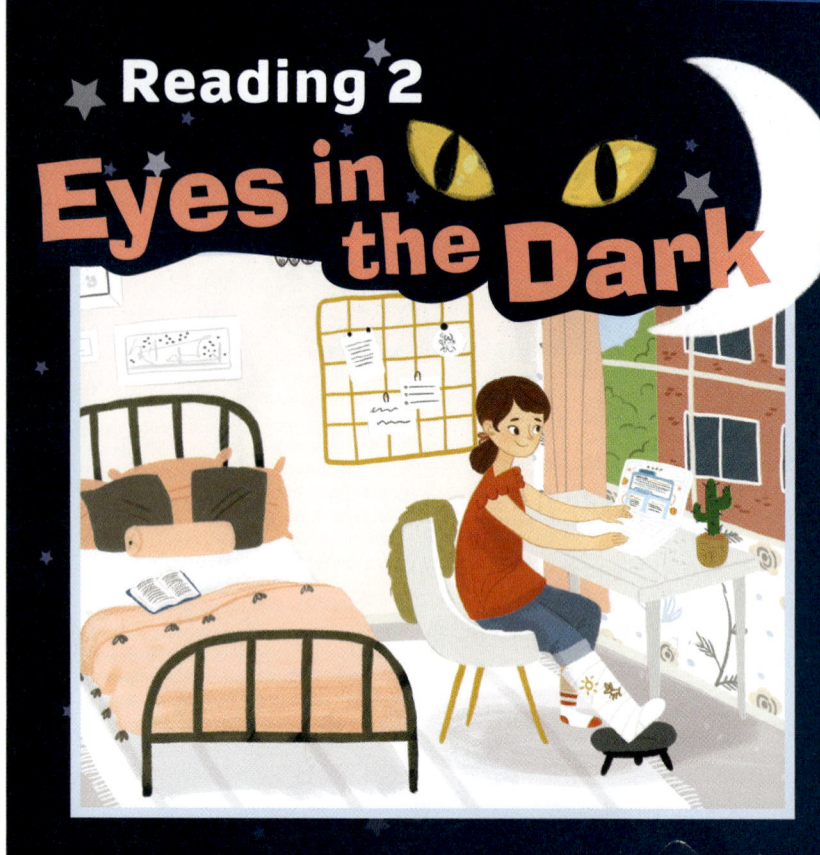

Reading 2

Eyes in the Dark

Hi, everyone! My name's Isabel and I'm a **blogger**. I love writing about what I've done, seen, or heard, and also about what I adore, can't stand, or don't mind. My mom reckons I'm the best **critic** … especially of her disgusting food! I don't think my **blog** will win any **awards**, but I may **inspire** you to start blogging.

July 30

Today has been horrible because I had an accident yesterday and broke my leg. 🦴 I'm now probably stuck in my room until it gets better. There's nothing to do except for blogging, reading, doing my homework, eating a bit of Mom's rock-hard meat loaf, and staring out the window at the birds. They're my only company … except for you, readers! Message me!

July 31

Today is my 11th birthday, and some of my friends came to visit. 🎂 We gossiped about school. You'll never guess what! Ms. Cross – the geography teacher – has had a baby girl. We also chatted about what's been happening at the shopping mall and a few things like that. Hey, my parents got me the most amazing thing ever – a 3D camera! Come back soon to see some totally cool pictures.

92

August 1
I didn't do anything this afternoon except for looking out of the window and "concentrating" on my biology homework. In the evening, however, something totally weird happened.
I saw something like a pair of eyes in the empty apartment across the street. What or who could they belong to? Message me if you know!

August 2
Another boring day of chemistry homework and horrible food, so thanks for your messages! They're totally **hilarious** and I'm happy to know you're reading and sending me your **entertaining** comments. 🙂 I'm not sure that those eyes belong to an alien, and I definitely don't think they belong to a robotic dog. But continue commenting with your suggestions.

August 3
The same thing happened tonight. While I was eating dinner (Mom's terrible spaghetti), I saw those strange eyes. Here's the picture. I told you I'd **post** some amazing pictures!

August 4
This is getting really creepy. There were two pairs of eyes in the apartment across the way tonight. They were looking directly at me. What do you think I should do everyone? Message me.

August 5
I'm so frightened because I think something terrible is happening. Tonight, there were four pairs of eyes in the apartment all looking directly at me. Here's the picture. I probably won't be able to sleep.

August 6
I had a visit from my friend, Aisha, who's a totally cool **writer**. She writes such amazing short stories and **articles** for the school **magazine**. We did a little literature and geography homework together and had such a good time. I showed her the pictures and she thinks I should call the police. Readers, let me know what I should do.

August 7
Mrs. Jones visited today, and she asked us if we'd seen her cat, Betsy. Betsy's been missing now for about a week and this has me thinking. I first saw the strange eyes six days ago. Could they belong to Betsy? But she only has two eyes. What about the other six? Message me your opinions!

August 8
Patricia from Orlando, I think you're the best! She believes I should tell Mrs. Jones all about the mysterious eyes. We may have found Betsy!

August 9
Today has been awesome. Mrs. Jones found her cat. And guess what! Betsy had three kittens. The extra eyes were theirs! Mrs. Jones thinks Betsy went into the apartment because she wanted somewhere secret and quiet to have her kittens. Mrs. Jones has also found a home for all the kittens! One is coming to live here with us, so now I have a pet cat! 🎉

4 Do you read blogs? What would you blog about?

Comprehension 2

1 Read *Eyes in the Dark* again and answer the questions.

1 On what days do you think Isabel was feeling bored? Why?

2 On what days do you think she was feeling excited? Why?

3 How was she feeling on August 4?

4 What events made Isabel feel happy?

2 Discuss with a friend. Then compare your answers with another pair.

1 Why do you think Isabel was bored with being stuck in her bedroom all the time?

2 Who or what did you think the mysterious eyes belonged to at first? Why did you think this?

3 What would you have done in the same situation?

4 Make up an alternative ending to the story.

3 How are blogs and diaries similar and different? Discuss with a friend.

Listening 2

4 Many people who learn a new language keep language diaries. How do you think this can help?

Listening strategy

Infer speakers' opinions in conversations on familiar everyday topics.

5 (2-10) Listen to the conversation between James and Samantha. Do they mention any of your ideas from Activity 4?

6 (2-11) Listen again. What does James think about language diaries at the start of the conversation? How does he feel about them at the end? How do you know?

7 Discuss with a friend.

1 In how many ways does the language diary help Samantha?

2 Which do you think is the most useful?

3 Which is the least useful?

8 A diary can be used to record our thoughts or to learn a language. What other ways can we use diaries? Discuss with a friend.

94

Vocabulary 2

1 Find these words in *Eyes in the Dark*. Then complete the chart.

> article   award   blog   blogger   concentrate   critic
> entertaining   hilarious   inspire   magazine   post   writer

Adjectives	Nouns	Verbs

2 Look at Activity 1. Which noun(s) can also be a verb? How is the meaning different?

3 🎧 2-12 Listen to the definitions. Write the words they refer to.

1 ....
2 ....
3 ....
4 ....
5 ....
6 ....
7 ....
8 ....
9 ....
10 ....
11 ....
12 ....

4 💬 Discuss with a friend.

1 Are you a blogger? If so, what do you blog about?
2 Do you read blogs? What blogs do you read?
3 Would you like to be a literary critic?
4 What kinds of literature do you find entertaining?

95

Grammar 2

1 Watch Part 2 of the story video again. Read and complete.

| minutes | sense | time |

At the start of Mr. Fisher's letter-writing class, Jade and Emily were bored. Then they did things differently. They wrote a letter together using one word at a time. At first, their letter made little ¹_____, but after a bit of ²_____ it became better. A few ³_____ later, the task was real fun.

2 Read the grammar box and complete. Then answer.

Grammar

a few, a little, a bit of

We use expressions like **a few**, **a little**, and **a bit of** when we want to talk about quantities of things.

I'll have **a little** sugar with my tea.
Can I add **a bit of** salt to this salad?
I made us **a few** sandwiches.

1. We use _____ with countable nouns.
2. We use _____ with uncountable nouns.
3. Do we use a singular noun or a plural noun after **a few**?

3 Read *Eyes in the Dark* again. Circle sentences with *a few*, *a little*, or *a bit of*.

4 Read and circle.

1. Jo has **a few** / **a bit of** dollars so she can buy a new T-shirt.
2. I need **a few** / **a little** glue to finish this project.
3. Can I have **a few** / **a little** candies, please?
4. I'll have **a few** / **a bit of** mayo on my hotdog.
5. Add **a few** / **a little** chilies to make your dish spicy.
6. There's **a few** / **a little** sand in my shoe.

5 Read and complete. Use *a few*, *a little*, or *a bit of*.

1 To make this dish, I should first mix .... milk, ... flour, and .... eggs.
2 Nadia is making a birthday card. She's putting .... stickers and .... glitter on it.
3 There's still .... water left in my drinking bottle and I still have .... apples.
4 My brother got .... money, so he bought himself .... fruit bars.

> We use **all of**, **most of**, and **none of** to talk about quantity.
>
> **All of** the people in the stadium are soccer fans. ●●●●●
> **Most of** them are fans of the blue team. ●●●○○
> **None of** them are fans of the yellow team. ○○○○○

6 Look at the picture and write what you see. Use the words from the box and *all of*, *most of*, or *none of*.

| blue uniforms | red uniforms | scarves |

1 ....
2 ....
3 ....

Speaking 2

7 💬 Think about the things your classmates do. Discuss with a friend. .

Some of our classmates play basketball.

None of them play chess.

But all of them play video games!

Writing

1 Read the book review. Answer the questions.

1 What's the text about?
2 Why does Julia like the book?

I Capture the Castle

by
Dodie Smith

Book review by
Julia Timpson

1 *I Capture the Castle* is a novel about a young girl called Cassandra Mortmain who decides to write about everything she sees and hears. It's an excellent book with a captivating plot.

2 Cassandra lives in a castle in England with her family. Their life changes when they meet another family, the Cottons. Her sister, Rose, and the neighbor boy, Simon, fall in love and decide to get married. Rose then starts to love Neil, Simon's brother, and they decide to run away. Cassandra discovers she has feelings for Simon.

3 The story is told from Cassandra's point of view and her narration is wonderful. She has many deep insights into her life and the life of others. *I Capture the Castle* is essential reading for anyone who loves fiction. This is because Dodie Smith's writing is superb and the story is engaging.

2 Read the book review again and write.

In which paragraph(s) does Julia …
1 give her opinion?
2 describe the characters?
3 give an introduction to the book?
4 describe the plot?

Writing strategy

Support a point of view with reasons and information in an opinion piece.
*This is the best book in the series **because** it has the best story.*

3 (WB 85) Think about a novel, a poem, or a comic book that you love. Then go to the Workbook to do the writing activity.

Now I Know

1 What's literature? Look back through Unit 6, remember what you learned, and make a list of all the different kinds of literature. Why do people use each kind?

....

....

....

2 Choose a project.

Make presentation slides with a profile of an author.

1. Think of an author you like.
2. Use the internet to research the author. Find out as much about them as possible.
3. Create presentation slides.
4. Present your profile to the class.

or

Write an article for the school magazine or school blog.

1. Think about what kind of article you're going to write.
2. Research the information that you need for your article.
3. Write your article for the school magazine or blog.

Self-assessment

Check (✔) or cross (✘) for you.

| ✘ I can't do this yet. | ✔ I can do this. | ✔✔ I liked doing this. |

I can understand the main points of an interview.

I can identify opinions.

I can compare information in different texts on the same topic.

I can make inferences about characters' motives and feelings.

I can give an opinion in a structured discussion.

I can talk about matters of personal interest.

I can write a review of a book.

7

How do we communicate?

Listening
- I can recognize linking words/phrases signaling the sequence of events.
- I can extract key details from extended monologs.

Reading
- I can scan texts on the same topic to find specfic information.
- I can follow the sequence of messages on social media.

Speaking
- I can make predictions about the future.
- I can answer questions about what I have done recently.

Writing
- I can write a story with a clear sequence of events.

1 💬 **Look at the picture and discuss.**

1 What's the girl holding?
2 Who's she talking to?
3 Why is she using technology?

2 💬 **Read and make notes. Then compare your answers with a friend.**

1 How do people send messages to each other?
2 How did people send messages in the past?
3 Which method is faster?

3 ▶ 7-1 BBC **Look at the video still and predict. What's the man doing?**

4 ▶ 7-1 BBC **Watch the video and check your answer from Activity 3. Then watch again and check (✔) the true sentences.**

1 Computers are capturing body movement to look for clues about human feelings. ☐
2 Computers don't have to learn about human emotions. ☐
3 Our face is the least expressive part of our body. ☐
4 Combinations of gestures help computers read human mental states. ☐
5 Human facial expressions are easy to read. ☐

Pre-reading 1

1 Discuss with a friend.

1. How many hours a day do you use a smartphone or tablet?
2. Which of the following uses of a smartphone/tablet are most important to you? Why?
   - social media
   - text messaging
   - phone and video calls
   - taking pictures
   - playing games

> **Reading strategy**
>
> Scan texts to find specific information.

2 Read. What percentage of young people spend more than eight hours a day online?

> Tanya Goodin, the founder of a digital detox company aimed at teenagers, took a survey of more than 500 young people aged 13 to 18. Of those, 29% said they spent more than eight hours a day online while 36% admitted they regularly fell asleep with their phone or laptop in bed. Two-thirds (67%) said they used their phone when they were bored and almost 60% revealed they used their phone in uncomfortable social situations.

3 2-13 Read Digital Detox. How many hours a day do they spend on their phones or tablets?

Reading 1

Digital Detox

Do you check your smartphone every five minutes? Do you speak more on FaceTime than you do **face-to-face**? Do you spend all your time on messaging apps? If you answered "yes", it sounds like you need a digital detox! We **persuaded** three teens to give up their smartphones and tablets for a week! Let's see how they got on.

> **The Rules**
> 1. No access to smartphones, tablets, or laptops
> 2. No TV
> 3. Only calls on landline phones permitted

Ben, 13, San Francisco, United States

I spend about five hours a day on my phone or tablet, mainly messaging my friends and playing video games. My mom **convinced** me to take part in the digital detox. At first, it was really difficult and I was really bored. I used my landline to call my best friend, but it was strange talking on the phone – you can't see the expression of the person you're speaking to. I had so much time on my hands that I decided to research old methods of **non-verbal** communication. To do my research I had to go to the library, of course! Native Americans used smoke signals to **communicate** over long distances and other ancient cultures used drums. My dad wasn't keen on me doing either of those in my bedroom! It was fun not using my phone. I might do another detox in the future.

Khadejah, 14, Vancouver, Canada

I use my phone all the time, about six hours a day. Even when my friends come to visit, we sit on our phones for **messaging** each other and other friends, and looking at social media. I think we've created a whole new language group with emojis and hashtags. But emojis can lead to more **misunderstanding** than **written** or verbal communication.

During my digital detox, I saw my friends face-to-face a lot more. I found myself using hand **gestures** more often during conversations to **express** myself. I even **imitated** emojis with facial expressions and did hashtag signs with my hands! It was liberating not to have my phone for a week. I definitely spent more time actually talking to my friends and family, and I did more homework! I was happy to get my phone back after the end of the week, but I won't use it as much as I did.

Lauren, 15, Austin, United States

I'm partially deaf, so messaging apps and FaceTime have been a breakthrough for me and the rest of the non-hearing world. I use my phone for at least four hours a day. Over the last 20 years, everyone has gone from verbal to more written forms of communication like email, SMS, and messaging apps – it's great for the deaf community!

I've never used a landline phone because I can't hear the replies very well. I use my smartphone to communicate with friends a lot. I use FaceTime with my non-deaf friends as I can lip-read and have a two-way conversation. I use sign language on FaceTime with my deaf friends. **Sign language** is a language for the deaf which uses hand gestures to represent letters and words. We use a lot of facial expressions as well to show emotions. During my detox week, I went out with friends a lot more. A group of teenagers not making any noise but all chatting away in sign language certainly gets attention!

I was so happy at the end of my digital detox week. I know teenagers are addicted to their phones, but I felt really isolated without mine.

4 What do you think would be the most difficult thing about a digital detox?

Comprehension 1

1 🗨 **Read *Digital Detox* again. Ask and answer with a friend.**

1. a How did Ben find the digital detox in the beginning?
   b Which key word(s) helped you find the answer?
2. a What did Khadejah do during her digital detox?
   b Which key word(s) helped you find the answer?
3. a What does Lauren never use?
   b Which key word(s) helped you find the answer?

2 **Who do you think says the following? Read and write *B* (Ben), *K* (Khadejah), or *L* (Lauren).**

1. Emojis can cause misunderstandings. I once used a crying-laughing emoji when I meant to use a crying-sad emoji, and my friend was really upset! ☐
2. Modern forms of written and audio-visual communication have been life-changing for people like me. ☐
3. Looking for answers in library books was fun, but a lot slower than Google! ☐

3 🗨 **Work in groups of three.**

1. Compare how much you use digital technology each day.
2. Discuss which member should do a digital detox.

Listening 1

4 🗨 **Without technology, how would you communicate with friends and family? Discuss with a friend.**

> 🎧 **Listening strategy**
>
> Listen for sequencers and dates to understand chronology.

5 🎧 2-14 **Listen. What was the first form of written communication?**

6 🎧 2-15 **Listen again. Number the forms of communication in chronological order and write the dates when they started.**

- Morse code .... ☐
- Cave painting .... ☐
- Chatrooms .... ☐
- Telephone .... ☐
- Pictograms .... ☐
- Blogs .... ☐

7 🗨 **Which forms of communication have you used? What advantages/disadvantages do they offer? Discuss with a friend.**

Vocabulary 1

1 Find these words in *Digital Detox*. Then complete the chart and write the verbs as nouns.

| communicate | convince | express | face-to-face | gesture | imitate |
| message | misunderstand | non-verbal | persuade | sign language | written |

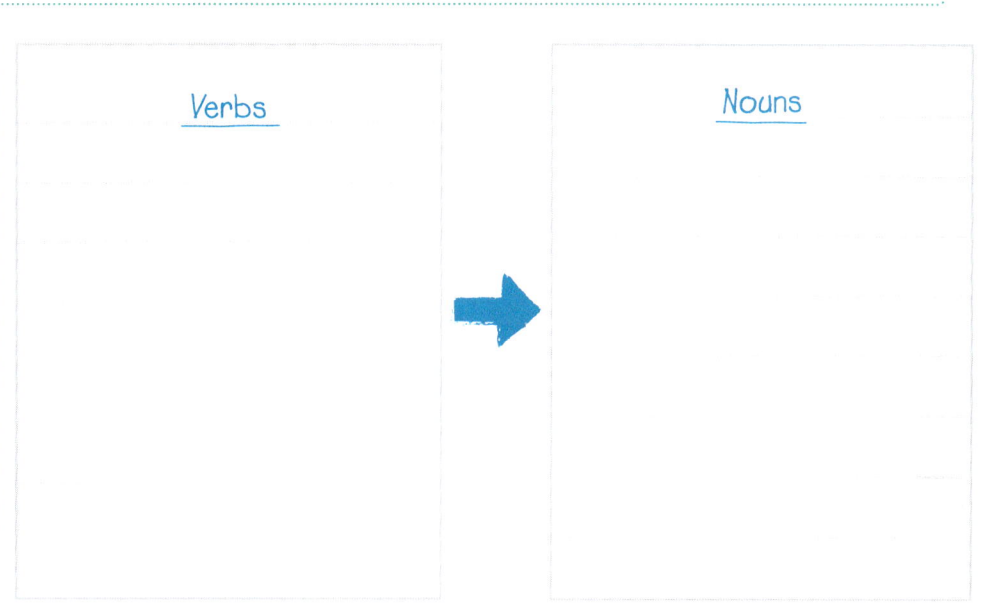

Ways to communicate	Verbs	➡ Nouns

2 🎧 2-16 Listen and say.

3 💬 Work in pairs. Brainstorm different kinds of communication.

Audio radio,
Visual blogs,
Audio-visual TV,

4 💬 When do you use different kinds of communication? Discuss with a friend.

> I use the landline telephone to speak to my grandma.

> Really? My grandma has a smartphone so we have video calls.

Grammar 1

1 Watch Parts 1 and 2 of the story video. Who are the two new people at school? What do Jade and Oli say? Read and complete.

You must speak to Ms. Sanches. She might have ....

She may not ....

2 Watch Part 2 of the story video again. What's Oli's problem? Check (✔).

1 He doesn't like the new boy. ☐
2 He doesn't know how to role-play. ☐
3 The role-play situation reflects his real-life situation. ☐

3 Read the grammar box and circle.

> **Grammar**
>
> **Future using may/might/will**
>
> In the future, people **might** travel to other planets. They **may not** write letters.
> I **won't** be available on Saturday. My sister **will** be there.
>
> 1 We use *may (not)* and *might (not)* to express **certainty** / **possibility** in the future.
> 2 We use *will* and *won't* to make predictions and express **certainty** / **possibility** for the future.

4 Read *Digital Detox* again. Circle sentences with *may*, *might*, and *will*.

5 Read and circle.

1 I definitely **will** / **won't** be able to come after school. I'm too busy.
2 Quick! If we leave now, we **won't** / **might** make it in time.
3 We **may not** / **'ll** meet you outside the shopping mall at 8 p.m. See you soon!
4 Mom says we **may** / **won't** have pizza for dinner, if we're good.

6 Look at the weather forecast. Read and complete.

Day	Weather	Probability
Friday	☀	100%
	💧	50%
Saturday	☀	20%
	💧	45%
Sunday	☀	0%
	❄	65%

1 On Friday, it _____ be sunny.
2 It _____ rain on Friday.
3 It _____ be sunny on Saturday.
4 It _____ rain on Saturday.
5 On Sunday, it _____ be sunny.
6 It _____ snow on Sunday.

7 Look at Hazel's possible plans for the weekend and complete.

This weekend I might _____ with my friends.
We _____ .
I _____ with my _____ .
We _____ .
I might not _____ .

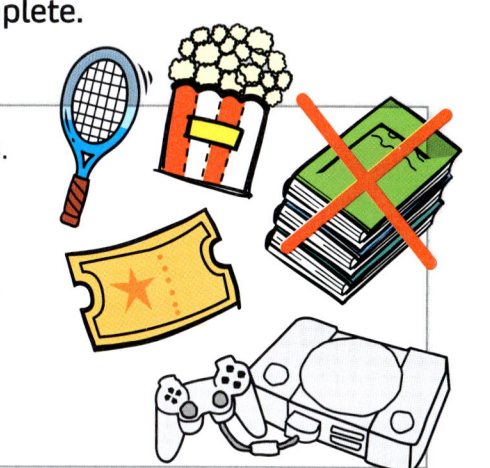

Speaking 1

8 🗨 What may be the future of communication? Discuss with a friend.

> We might send hologram messages.

> I didn't think of that. Also, we might not use cell phones.

Speaking strategy

Use phrases like *I thought so, too* and *I didn't think of that* to compare ideas.

Pre-reading 2

1 Think about the last message you wrote. Discuss with a friend.

1. Who did you message?
2. What did you talk about?

> **Reading strategy**
> Pay attention to settings or events.

2 Read the messages. Why do you think they decide to meet face-to-face?

> The most amazing thing happened this morning.

> What?! Tell me!

> So, I was visiting my friend Sara and I got talking to her dad.

> Is that the friendly guy with a beard? 🧔

> Yes! He's a film director, he's directed all sorts of really cool films!

> ...

> I tell you what, Marta – shall we meet face-to-face so I can tell you properly?

3 Read *Head Boy Hearing*. How many different people message? Who writes the last message?

Reading 2
Head Boy Hearing

Well, this is **awkward**. I'm Ben Bradley, Head Boy of Carlton Academy 2036–2037 and captain of the Hover Board Hockey Team, and I'm waiting for my hearing in front of the virtual school council. I find myself accused of vandalism. There is a new **unfriendly** system at school where any serious disciplinary matters are decided by the virtual school council online. I must **represent** myself in writing, which is a shame as I can't use my charm and humorous **conversation** skills. The school council site flashes on my laptop. My hearing is about to go live. I suddenly feel quite **emotional** about the situation.
beep

Virtual school council hearing #043 Ben Bradley

> OK, here we go. 500 words just aren't enough to prove I didn't do this, and I'm already down to 479. Well, my name is Ben Bradley as you already know. I'm Head Boy. I'm innocent.

> **@JJ_Bee** We've all read the evidence already. We know that a can of spray paint was found in your locker. I think you're #guilty.

> Please don't use up my words. Now I've only got 429 left. I need my words. I'm Head Boy. I'm captain of the Hover Board Hockey Team. Why would I want to vandalise the changing rooms? And why would I throw my own Hover Board through a window? Seriously?

> **@Amol_Chandra** We've got eye-witness accounts and CCTV images showing you running from the scene. #guilty

7

Please, please – if your choice is guilty, make that all you say. My words are precious. Don't use up my words and waste my hearing time. This system is ridiculous.

@**Teacher_Chair** Let's keep to the point, please. If we **collaborate**, we can get through this quickly.

@**Gregory.Adams** You're not even trying to make an **argument**. I'm **speechless**. #guilty

Greg, listen to me – I know that you're an educated student, so listen to the truth. I never mentioned this before. I was protecting him – my brother, Cal. I love my brother, but he's jealous of me. He wants to be the captain of the Hover Board Hockey Team and wants me out of the way. Do you understand what happens to me if there are more guilties than innocents? I will be suspended from school. I'll lose the title of Head Boy. I'll lose the scholarship I have to the best college in the country. That will harm my whole future! And, worst of all, without me the Hover Board Hockey Team won't win the Tri-County School's Cup for the first time in four years!

@**RyanRox** I believe you're being **dishonest**, but I don't want our team to start losing – you're a good captain! #innocent

Thank you, but I DIDN'T do it. It was my brother, Cal Bradley. He put the spray paint in my locker. It's his image on the CCTV.

@**Rosie_Red** Ben, I've seen your brother. He does resemble you with his hair style and clothes. I think you are #innocent.

Anyone else? Anyone else to vote innocent? And please save my words.

@**Zu_Chan** I agree with @Rosie_Red – your brother does look really like you. And I know what his **behaviour** can be like sometimes. #innocent

YES! It's a draw. That's a draw, right? So I can **request** a second **hearing**, can't I? Then I can bring in the evidence against Cal. Oh YES! Thank you @RyanRox, @Rosie_Red, and @Zu_Chan. You guys have saved my future! 453 words. Nearly there. Is there anyone else online? Anyone want to give me another #innocent to save us from a retrial?

@**Teacher_Chair** Anyone?

OK. I'll quickly use up my word limit since we're not quite there yet blah blah blah 494 blah blah 497 blah.

@**Cal_Bradley** #guilty, brother.

4 Do you think this form of communication might be used in the future for trials and hearings? Why?

109

Comprehension 2

1 Read *Head Boy Hearing* again and answer the questions.

1 What was the verdict of the first three people to post responses?
2 Who was the first person to give a #innocent verdict?
3 Apart from Ben, which other person didn't give a verdict?

2 Read and complete.

> Thank you for taking part in the student council hearing #043 of Ben Bradley. Before any further action can be taken against the defendant, we need you to resubmit your verdict with a reason.
>
> @RyanRox # *innocent*
> Reason:
>
> @Gregory.Adams #
> Reason:
>
> @Amol_Chandra #
> Reason:
>
> @Zu_Chan #
> Reason:
>
> @Cal_Bradley #
> Reason:
>
> @JJ_Bee #
> Reason:
>
> @Rosie_Red #
> Reason:

3 Listen to the school principal and @Teacher_Chair discussing the hearing. Check your answers from Activity 2. (2-18)

Listening 2

4 Have you ever written a poem? Why do you think people write poetry?

> 🎧 **Listening strategy**
>
> Follow an audio presentation of a poem.

5 Listen. What's the poem about? (2-19)

6 Listen again. Write the different things the author does on the phone. Compare with a friend. (2-20)

7 Discuss the poem with a friend.

1 What do you think it means?
2 How does it make you feel?
3 What does communication mean to you?

110

Vocabulary 2

1 Find these words in *Head Boy Hearing*. Then write a synonym for each word. Use a dictionary or a thesaurus.

1. conversation (n) ....
2. speechless (adj) ....
3. emotional (adj) ....
4. represent (v) ....
5. behavior (n) ....
6. collaborate (v) ....
7. argument (n) ....
8. awkward (adj) ....
9. request (v) ....
10. unfriendly (adj) ....
11. hearing (n) ....
12. dishonest (adj) ....

2 🎧 2-21 Listen to synonyms of the words from Activity 1. Which words do they refer to? Work with a friend.

🇬🇧 British	🇺🇸 American
behaviour	behavior

3 Match the symbols to their names and uses on social media.

1	@	emoji	precedes a word or phrase to give topic headings
2	#	dot	used in email addresses and social media user names
3	🙂	hashtag	separates a website's name from its domain (it's a period, but for internet use we say *dot*)
4	.	at	a little picture that shows an emotion or illustrates a topic of conversation

4 Write a social media chat with a friend. Include words and symbols from this lesson.

111

Grammar 2

1 Watch Part 2 of the story video again. What does Jade say? Read and complete.

We can meet in the library café. I've .... there before.

2 Read the grammar box and complete.

> **Grammar**
>
> **Present Perfect with *already* and *yet***
>
> Has she finished **yet**?
> She hasn't finished **yet**.
> I've **already** finished!
>
> .... is used in affirmative sentences.
> **Yet** is used in .... and negative sentences.

3 Read *Head Boy Hearing* again. Circle sentences with *already* or *yet*.

4 Read and complete. Use *already* or *yet*.

1. Have we finished the experiment .... ?
2. I've .... finished all my homework for today.
3. We haven't started the exam ....
4. My brother hasn't come back from school ....
5. Have you been to the new skate park .... ?
6. Arthur has .... eaten his lunch.

5 Write the words in order to make sentences. Use correct punctuation.

1 called / Terri / Grandma / yet / has

   ....

2 she / yet / the / answered / hasn't / phone

   ....

3 emails / I've / today / already / three / sent

   ....

4 yet / have / your / posted / blog / you

   ....

6 Look at the pictures and write. Use *already* or *yet*.

1 **Lucy:** ....
   Mark: No, I haven't.

2 **Emma:** Has Rania finished playing basketball?
   Tony: No, ...

3 **Rick:** Do you need to do any homework?
   Sam: No, I don't. ....

Speaking 2

7 Look at the to-do list of tasks on a school day. Check (✓) what you have already done. Add three more tasks that you haven't done yet.

8 💬 Look at the list from Activity 7. Ask and answer with a friend. Make questions with *yet* and answer with *already* or *yet*.

To-do list

1 send Mom a text ☐
2 have lunch ☐
3 do homework ☐
4 ....
5 ....
6 ....

> Have you met your new teacher yet?

> Yes, I've met her twice already. Have you had lunch yet?

> No, I haven't had it yet.

113

Writing

1 Read the story. Is it set in the past or the present?

A Letter in a Bottle

Paul was feeling very emotional. If only there was a way he could contact his father. But it was impossible – his dad was already thousands of kilometers away on the other side of the ocean. Paul, his mother, and his little sisters were going to make the long voyage to Australia to join their father, but they couldn't go yet. Their ship was leaving in two months. Paul decided to write in a letter everything he wanted to say to his dad; how much he missed him, how excited he was to see him again, and how he'd already grown two inches since he last saw him.

Paul rolled up his little letter, put it in a small bottle, and put the cork in very tightly. He ran down to the beach and threw the bottle into the ocean.

Years later, Paul and his father were walking along the beach. Paul saw something shiny in the waves. It was the letter he wrote all those years ago!

2 Read the story again and answer.

1 **Beginning:** Is Paul younger at the beginning or the end of the story?
2 **Middle:** What object is used to focus the reader's attention?
3 **End:** How does this object link earlier and later events?

Writing strategy

Organize an event sequence that unfolds naturally in a story.
Forty years later, Laurie was waiting …

3 Brainstorm ideas for your own story. Organize them in a mind map. Then go to the Workbook to do the writing activity.

Now I Know

1 How do we communicate? Look back through Unit 7, remember what you learned, and write.

....
....
....

2 Choose a project.

Research communication in the past.

1 Use books or the internet to research past forms of communication.
2 Create an infographic or a timeline about the history of communication.
3 Present your research to the class.

or

Make a form of communication.

1 Work with a friend. Imagine you're in apartments on either side of the street. You can see each other but you can't hear each other. You can't use any modern technology.
2 Think of a way you can communicate. For non-verbal communication, write a language or code.
3 Try out your communication method.

Self-assessment

Check (✔) or cross (✘) for you.

✘ I can't do this yet. ✔ I can do this. ✔✔ I liked doing this.

I can recognize linking words/phrases signaling the sequence of events.
I can extract key details from extended monologs.
I can scan texts on the same topic to find specfic information.
I can follow the sequence of messages on social media.
I can make predictions about the future.
I can answer questions about what I have done recently.
I can write a story with a clear sequence of events.

8

How are things made by hand?

Listening
- I can understand details in extended dialogs.
- I can recognize linking words/phrases signaling the sequence of events.

Reading
- I can compare information in different texts on the same topic.
- I can understand the main information of a process.

Speaking
- I can summarize key information.

Writing
- I can introduce additional information.

1 💬 Look at the picture and discuss.

1 What do you think she's making? What materials is she using?
2 Do you know anyone who makes things by hand? What do they make?

2 💬 Think of things you have at home and school. Make notes. Then compare your answers with a friend.

Handmade	Mass-produced

3 ▶ 8-1 BBC Look at the video still and predict. What's he going to make?

4 ▶ 8-1 BBC Watch the video and check your answer from Activity 3. Then watch again and answer the questions.

1 What does he use these things for?
   a CD case   c bubble wrap
   b cereal box d polystyrene ball
2 Why does he mix paint with PVA glue?
3 Have you made a puppet before? How?

117

Pre-reading 1

1 💬 Discuss with a friend.

1 Think of two stories you know with similar topics or themes.
2 Compare and contrast the stories with a friend.
3 Share your ideas with the class.

> 📖 **Reading strategy**
>
> Compare and contrast the treatment of similar themes and topics in stories.

2 Read. What do you think the narrator knits?

> My little sister is three and she has a toy she carries everywhere. My sister's toy is a blue rabbit my grandma knitted. My grandma died last year, so I don't think my sister remembers her. One day we went on a boat trip. My little sister got so excited that she started jumping up and down. My mom grabbed her, but the rabbit fell into the ocean. We were all so upset! When we got home I found my grandma's knitting needles and yarn, and I watched videos to learn how to knit.

3 🎧 2-22 Read *The Blue Ribbon*. What does Mina make?

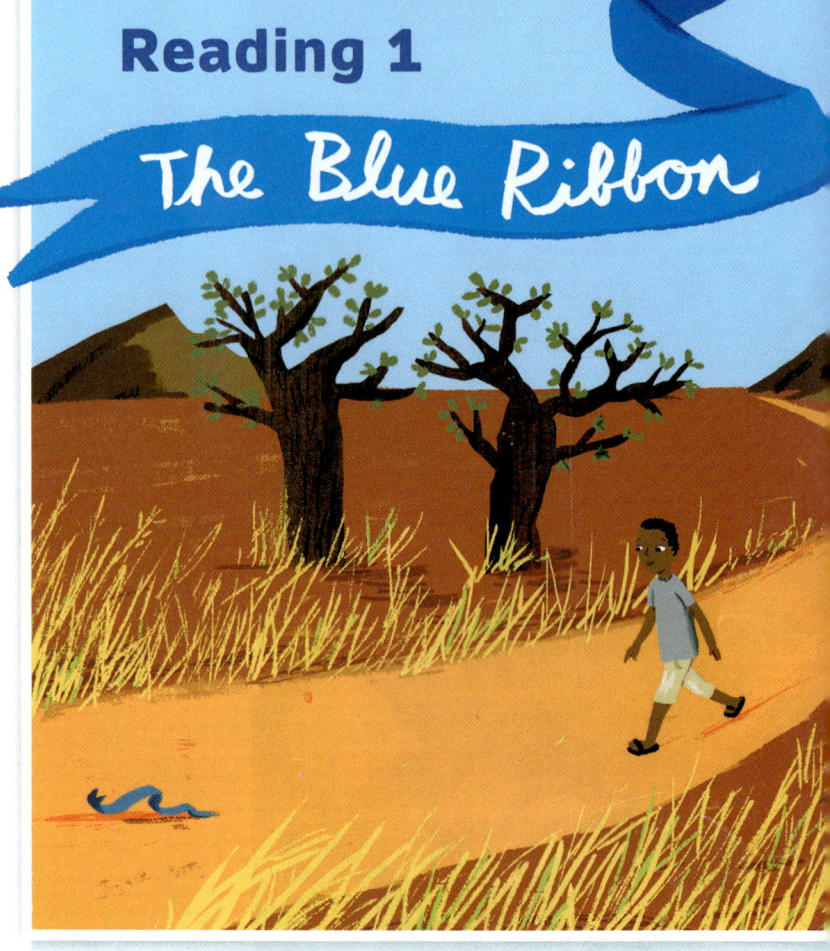

Reading 1

The Blue Ribbon

There's a man in a land far, far away who makes the most delicate blue ribbon. It's made of the finest, softest silk and sold all over the world. The people who buy it sew it onto dresses, cushions, quilts, and pillows. Legend has it that anything made from the blue ribbon brings success and happiness. Once a year, when the westerly winds blow, off-cuts of his ribbon are swept up into the sky and float gently away, like soft waves on the ocean.

In Botswana, there lived a boy named Baboloki. He walked for a whole hour just to get to school on time. He was often lonely and never had company on his journey. Baboloki studied **carpentry** and **sculpture**, but he couldn't afford all the tools. One day a cooling soft **breeze** blew through the warm air. A piece of blue ribbon came floating over the dirt track. It seemed to have a nice glow to it, so Baboloki reached up and grabbed it. The school bell sounded in the distance.

Baboloki selected his tools for woodshop class – a small hammer and an old **chisel** – and started to chip away at a piece of wood. His assignment for the day was to finish and polish a stool. He suddenly remembered he had the blue ribbon in his pocket. As he took it out to admire it, it fluttered out of his hand and landed on some mud a small distance away. He felt it was the only special thing he had, so he quickly jumped down and retrieved the ribbon. Then he saw something gleaming brightly. It was a set of shiny sculpting tools! Baboloki returned home happy, showing the tools to his father, a carpenter. That evening, he looked for his blue ribbon on the window sill, but it was floating away on the soft breeze.

In a wooden house in Mumbai, eleven-year-old Mina sleepily opened her eyes long before sunrise. Mina got up at 6 a.m. to fetch spring water from a memorial statue to add to the ground oats and rice she had for breakfast. Then at 7 a.m. Mina set off to the tailoring school where she would make **garments**.

A strip of blue ribbon made of silk fluttered over the Indian Ocean. It floated lightly in the air and landed at Mina's feet as she walked to school. She picked it up and tied it around her long plait. At school, her little fingers **expertly** guided the **needle** to **stitch** shiny **beads** and **sequins**, and add **embroidery** onto T-shirts and dresses. The last items she made by hand that day were sandals which she made by **skilfully** plaiting ribbons, leather, and beads. The colorful ribbons reminded her of the beautiful blue ribbon in her hair. As she walked home tired after a long day, she took the ribbon out of her hair to admire. A breeze blew it from her fingers and Mina followed it to the pile of trash where it landed. Something under the ribbon caught her eye. She pulled back the garbage and saw a small leather bag. She looked inside. It was full of rupee bills! Money! Mina looked around nervously. No one had noticed.

Mina tied the ribbon back in her hair and put the bag in her backpack, excited about telling her family about it. Later that evening she remembered her ribbon, but it had slipped away from her hair.

In the south of China, in the city of Gwangzhou, Jia is rushing to get to art school. Suddenly, a flash of blue catches his eye …

4 What do you think happens to Jia?

Comprehension 1

1 Read *The Blue Ribbon* again and remember *The House of the Jaguar* from Unit 2. Compare and contrast style and themes.

1   *The Blue Ribbon*

    ....

2   *The House of the Jaguar*

    ....

3   Shared themes

    ....

2 Read and write *B* (Baboloki) and/or *M* (Mina).

1   Who lives in a wooden house?
2   Who lives a long way from their school?
3   Who uses tools at school?
4   Who uses their hands to make things?
5   Who works with shiny things?
6   Who finds money?

3 Work in groups of four. Answer the questions. Take turns answering the questions in a different way.

1   How do you think Baboloki's story continues?
2   How do you think Mina's story continues?

Listening 1

4 Remember when a friend told you an exciting story. Which words did he/she use to describe emotions?

> **Listening strategy**
>
> Recognize words describing feelings and emotions.

5 Listen. Which of the children from *The Blue Ribbon* is speaking? (2-23)

6 Listen again and answer. (2-24)

1   How does her mother feel about the money? Why?

2   How does Mina feel about the blue ribbon?

3   How do you think they feel when they walk past the tailoring school the next day?

7 Think about Mina's story. Were any of your ideas from Activity 3 correct? Do you think she did the right thing?

Vocabulary 1

1 Find these words in *The Blue Ribbon*. What does each word mean?

bead ☐   chisel ☐   expertly ☐   needle ☐   sequin ☐   skilfully ☐
carpentry ☐   embroidery ☐   garment ☐   breeze ☐   sculpture ☐   stitch ☐

2 Look at Activity 1. How did you figure out the meaning of each word? Number the techniques you used.

1. I already knew the word.
2. It's similar to a word in my own language.
3. I used the context of the word.
4. I used the pictures.
5. I used a dictionary.

3 💬 Work with a friend. Compare your definitions to the words. Then check in a dictionary.

4 List the adverbs from Activity 1. Then find more adverbs in *The Blue Ribbon*. Write the root of each word.

> **Tip**
> The root word is the shortest form of a word. It can be a noun, adjective, or verb.

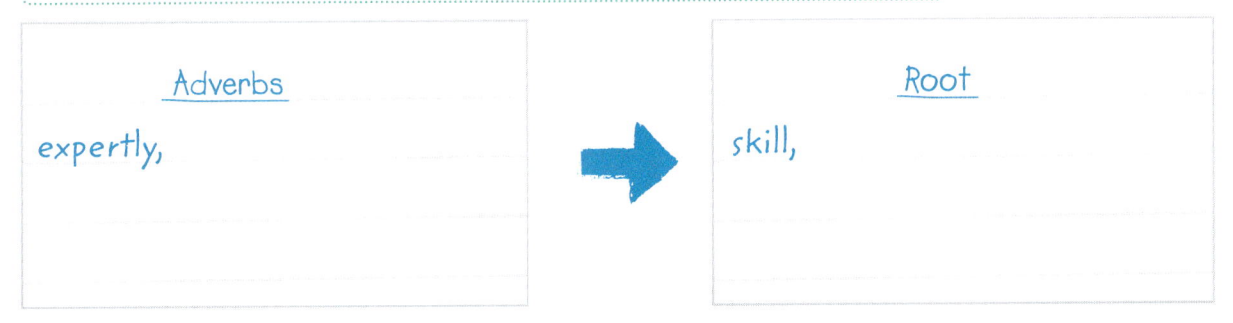

Adverbs	→	Root
expertly,		skill,

5 💬 Play *Word Association* with a friend.

1. Start each time with a word from this lesson.
2. Take turns saying a word you associate with the previous word.
3. Continue until one of you pauses or repeats a word.

Grammar 1

1 Watch Part 1 of the story video. What ideas does each of Jade's classmates have? Read and complete.

- made of wood
- made of paper
- made of wool
- made of metal
- made of card
- made of plastic

First, we looked at some things _____ wood.

2 Read the grammar box and complete.

Grammar

made of, made from, made by

The notebook is **made of** paper.
Plastic is **made from** oil.
The jewelry is **made by** hand.

We use **made** _____ to talk about how or who made something.
We use **made** _____ to talk about the basic material.
We use **made** _____ to talk about how something is manufactured.

3 Read *The Blue Ribbon* again. Circle sentences with *made of*, *made from*, or *made by*.

4 Read and complete. Use *of*, *from*, or *by*.

1. Paper is made _____ wood.
2. Glass is made _____ sand.
3. Garments are made _____ tailors.
4. My shoes are made _____ leather.
5. My aunt's antique desk is made _____ oak.
6. Alicia's dress was made _____ her mom.

122

5 Look at the objects and write what they are made of.

1   It's made ....

2   It's ....

3   ....

4   ....

Speaking 1

6 Think of an object. Complete the word web.

> **Speaking strategy**
> Use words like *OK* and *so* to link answers and questions.

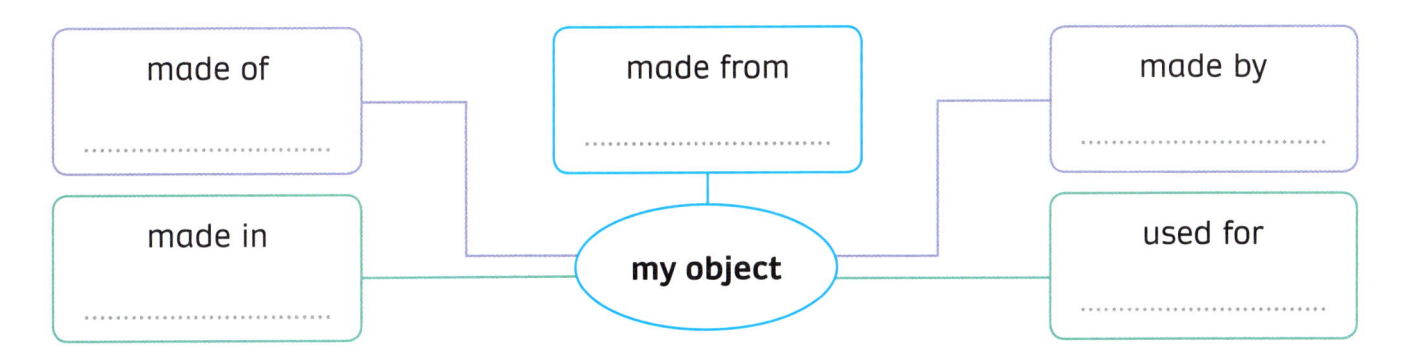

| made of | made from | made by |
| made in | my object | used for |

7 Work with a friend. Take turns asking and answering to guess the object from Activity 6.

1   You can only ask questions with the answer *yes* or *no*.
2   You can only ask 10 questions before you guess what the object is.

Is it made of paper?

No, it isn't.

OK. So, is it made of wood?

123

Pre-reading 2

1 💬 Think of something that you have made by hand. Discuss with a friend.

1. Tell your friend how you make your chosen item but don't tell him/her what it is.
2. See if your friend can guess what it is you're talking about from your instructions.

> 📖 **Reading strategy**
>
> Interpret information in illustrated instructions.

2 💡 Look at the pictures below. What are the instructions for? Read and check your answer.

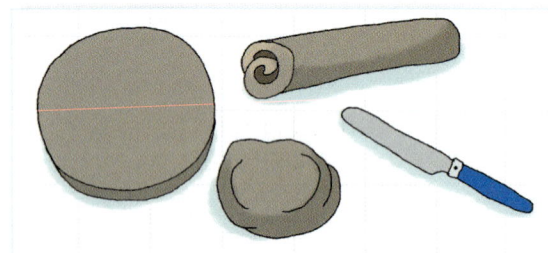

Start out with a round base about 10 mm thick. Then form clay rolls with your fingers spread, rolling them along your work surface.
Place the first coil around the outside of your base and give it a few taps with a flat knife to help the clay adhere to the base below it, and then smooth both the inside and outside of the coil into the base so it forms a smoothly contoured surface.

3 🎧 2-25 Look at the images in *Origami Bird* without reading the text. How do you think the bird is made? Then read.

Reading 2

Claudia's Bird Board

Hi! I'm Claudia – welcome to my board! It's all about my two favourite things: birds and making things!

Garden Bird Box

A bird box is an amazing addition to your garden. Especially if, like me, you want to encourage birds! Making a **homemade** bird box means that you can make it specifically to attract the type of birds you want to see. Now let's put your box together!

① First, cut out six pieces of wood using a **saw**, and sand or **file** the sawn **edges** to make them smooth.

② Then use a flat wood **drill** bit to drill the hole in the front panel and drill pilot holes for screws.

③ After that, use a screwdriver, either mechanical or manual, to **screw** in the screws and join the pieces together.

④ Finally, drill two 8 mm holes in the top corners of the back of the bird box. These holes will allow you to hang your bird box from a tree or fence.

⑤ Don't be tempted to **hammer** your bird box directly to a tree. The tree will grow and stretch the nails which will split the wood. Use the holes you have drilled in the back to tie some cord to the box and to the tree.

⑥ Don't worry if all the parts of your box do not fit together. Carpentry is a very specialised skill and trust me, the birds won't mind if some of the joints do not line up perfectly!

Origami Bird

Do you prefer **craft** to carpentry? If so, you can **attempt** your own birds to decorate your bedroom. I love these origami birds and it won't surprise you to know that I've got them pinned up all over my bedroom! Did you know that the name *origami* comes from the Japanese words *ori* meaning "to fold" and *kami* meaning "paper"? It's a really literal name as that's exactly what it is – folding paper! Origami birds with wings are usually more complex than this, but this bird is very easy to **fold**. It only takes a few simple steps and the result is almost as awesome as the more complex ones.

Step 1:
Start with a square piece of origami paper. Fold the paper in half by folding the top corner to the bottom corner. You should have an **upside-down** triangle.

Step 2:
Fold part of the top down so that the edge is about halfway down. Don't make this flap too thin because this will become the wings.

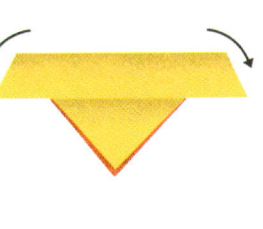

Step 3:
Turn the paper over.

Step 4:
Take the bottom corner of the top layer and fold it up.

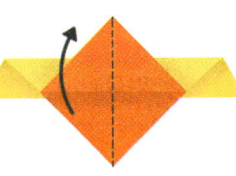

Step 5:
Fold the figure in half by folding the left side over to the right.

Step 6:
Now fold that same flap back like this to make one of the wings and do the same on the other side.

Step 7:
Push the centre of the head in and **flatten**. This is called an inside reverse fold.

Step 8:
And ta-da! You've made yourself a bird. Now set it free! Just kidding. Don't throw it in the air, it will just fall down and you'll be disappointed.

4 Which design do you want to make? Why?

125

Comprehension 2

1 Make the origami bird. Then answer the questions.

1 What helped you most to make it: the text or the pictures?
2 Does your finished design look correct?

2 Read *Claudia's Bird Board* again and answer the questions.

1 Why is it good to build a bird box yourself?

2 Why shouldn't you nail the box directly to a tree?

3 Where does origami originate from?

4 What does *origami* mean?

3 Think of something you make out of paper. Write instructions.

1 Brainstorm things you can make out of paper, e.g. paper planes, snowflakes, cootie catchers, etc.
2 Choose one you know how to make well. Write and illustrate instructions.
3 Swap instructions with a friend and make each other's design.

Listening 2

4 What words do you use when you want to give instructions?

Listening strategy
Understand the sequence of instructions from sequencing words.

5 Listen. What are the instructions for?
(2-26)

6 Listen again. Number the steps in order.
(2-27)

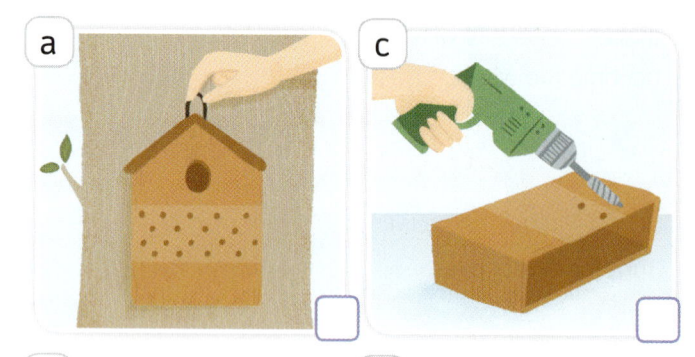

a
b
c
d

7 Discuss with a friend.

1 Why are some insects beneficial?
2 Where should you put a bug hotel?

126

Vocabulary 2

1 Complete the chart. Then circle the tools.

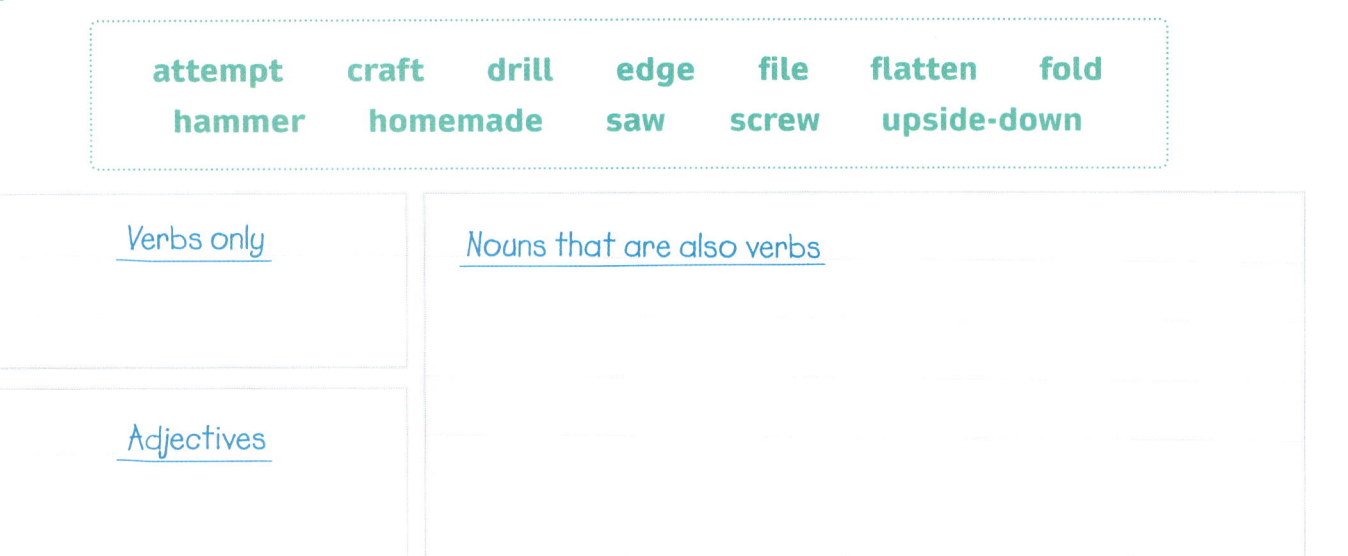

> attempt   craft   drill   edge   file   flatten   fold
> hammer   homemade   saw   screw   upside-down

Verbs only	Nouns that are also verbs

Adjectives	

2 Write the tools from Activity 1 next to their uses.

1. It smooths rough surfaces. _____
2. It cuts pieces of wood or metal. _____
3. It drives nails into wood. _____
4. It makes holes in wood or metal. _____
5. It joins pieces of wood together. _____

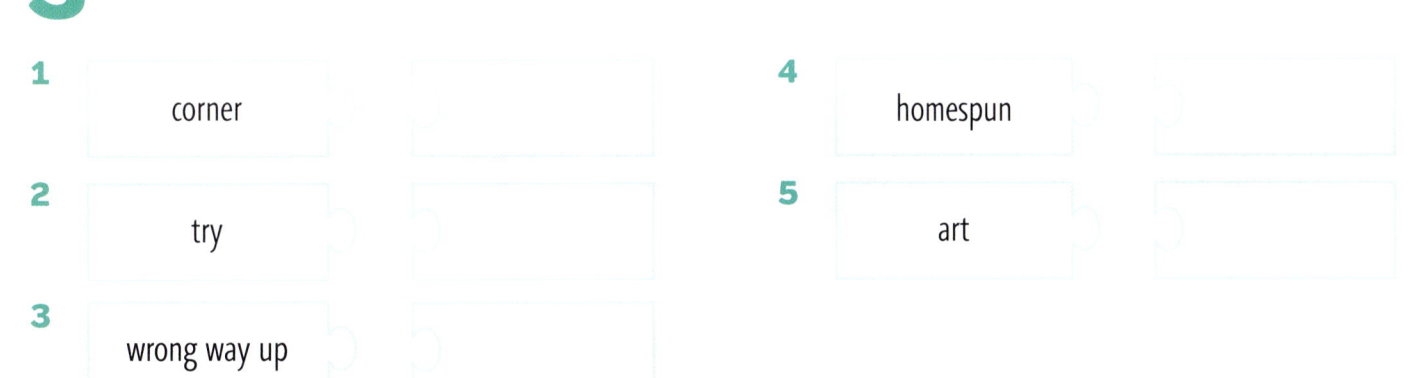

3 Write synonyms. Use the words from Activity 1.

1. corner — _____
2. try — _____
3. wrong way up — _____
4. homespun — _____
5. art — _____

4 Imagine you're making a wooden ship. What tools will you need? What steps should you take?

Grammar 2

1 Watch Part 2 of the story video. What happened in the art lesson?

2 Read the grammar box and complete.

Grammar

Present Simple for future

We use **Present Simple** for the future when events are routine or scheduled at a specific time.

My train **leaves** tomorrow at 5 p.m.
1 What time _____ the store close?
2 The store doesn't _____ until 7 p.m.

3 Read and complete the sentences.

1 The concert _____ at 8 p.m. (start)
2 What time _____ school _____ today? (end)
3 The shopping mall _____ until 7 a.m. (not open)
4 We have time. Dad's train _____ until 5 p.m. (not arrive)
5 Quick! The ticket office _____ at 6 p.m. (close)
6 When _____ the plane from Toronto _____ ? (land)

4 Look and write.

The bus _____

The train _____

5 Think about your town or city. Write about scheduled events.

1 The bus to school leaves at ....
2 The movie theater opens ....
3 ....
4 ....
5 ....

Speaking 2

6 Work with a friend. Design an airport schedule.

✈ Departures

To	Time
New York	1:15 p.m.
Mexico City	....
London	....
....	5:00 a.m.
....	11:45 a.m.

✈ Arrivals

From	Time
Seoul	....
Manila	3:20 p.m.
Perth	1:50 a.m.
....	....

7 Work with a friend. Take turns asking and answering questions using the airport schedule.

What time does the plane to New York depart?

What time does the plane from Perth land?

It departs at 1:15 p.m. We need to hurry up!

It lands at 1:50 a.m.

129

Writing

1 Read the flyer and answer the questions.

1 What time do the stalls open on Saturday?
2 What can you buy at the market?

HANDMADE ARTS AND CRAFTS MARKET

This weekend the streets of New Ville will be host to the Arts and Crafts Market! There will be over 30 stalls selling all sorts of handmade and artisan goods.

Here are a few:

Marco is selling his handmade furniture made of oak or pine.

Silvia makes beautiful hand-stitched beaded dresses, T-shirts, and skirts. She sells silk scarves as well.

You will also find artisan jewelry, handmade by Hamed. He's giving jewelry making demonstrations, too!

There will also be ceramics and origami workshops, leather bags and shoes, lamps, and many homemade food stalls!

Stalls open at 10 a.m. and close at 10 p.m. on Saturday, and are open from 12 p.m. till 8 p.m. on Sunday.

DON'T MISS IT!

Writing strategy

Use *also*, *as well*, and *too* when adding more information.
She found out that he does ballet **as well**.

2 Read the flyer again and circle.

1 We put *also* …
   a at the end of a sentence.   b at the beginning of a sentence.   c before the main verb.

2 We put *too* …
   a at the end of a sentence.   b at the beginning of a sentence.   c before the main verb.

3 We put *as well* …
   a at the end of a sentence.   b at the beginning of a sentence.   c before the main verb.

3 (WB 113) Go online and find out about a local weekend event. Then go to the Workbook to do the writing activity.

Now I Know

1 How are things made by hand? Look back through Unit 8, remember what you learned, and complete the lists.

What we use	What we make things with	How we make things	Finished products
needles,	silk,	skillfully,	garments,

2 Choose a project.

Interview a family member about something they made by hand.

1. Think of someone you know who has made something by hand.
2. Prepare interview questions and interview them.
3. Take a picture of their creation.
4. Write about your interview.

or

Design an item of your choice.

1. Choose an item to make, e.g. a toy, a garment, jewelry, or furniture.
2. Draw your design.
3. Think about the tools and materials you will use.
4. Write and illustrate the steps.

Self-assessment

Check (✔) or cross (✘) for you.

✘ I can't do this yet.   ✔ I can do this.   ✔✔ I liked doing this.

I can understand details in extended dialogs.

I can recognize linking words/phrases signaling the sequence of events.

I can compare information in different texts on the same topic.

I can understand the main information of a process.

I can summarize key information.

I can introduce additional information.

9

Why do we play sports?

Listening
- I can identify opinions.
- I can understand the main points of an interview.

Reading
- I can distinguish between fact and opinion.
- I can indentify the key characteristics of texts.

Speaking
- I can talk about matters of personal interest.
- I can describe past events, using descriptive language to add interest.

Writing
- I can show similarity between two ideas.

1 Look at the picture and discuss.

1. What's this person doing?
2. What's the name of the sport?
3. Do you think it's dangerous?

2 Read and make notes. Then compare your answers with a friend.

1. Would you like to do this sport?
2. Have you ever done any sports like this?
3. What sports do you think are the best for your body?

3 9-1 BBC Look at the video still and predict. What do you think this image represents?

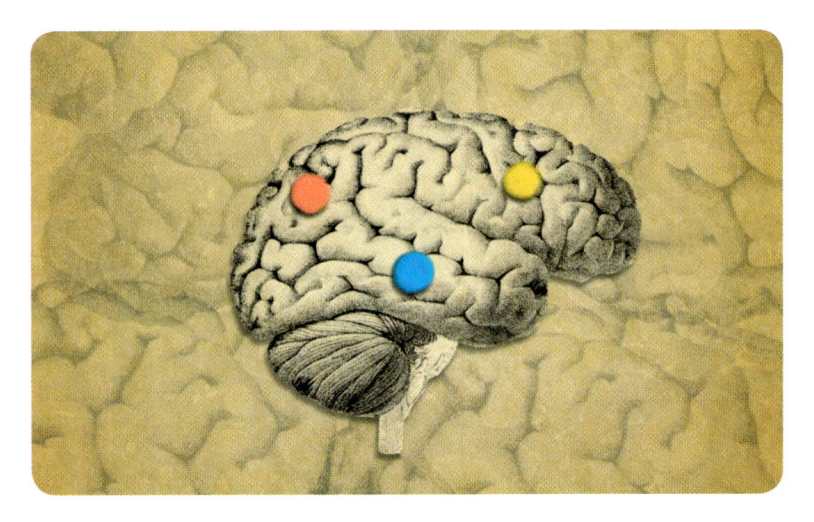

4 9-1 BBC Watch the video and check your answer from Activity 3. Then watch again and answer the questions.

1. Why can exercising be good at exam time?
2. How is exercising similar to laughing?
3. What's a good way to get motivated?
4. What exercise can you do if the weather's bad?
5. What can make you feel tired: too much exercise, too little exercise, or both?

133

Pre-reading 1

1 💬 Discuss with a friend. Then share with the class.

1 Choose a sport.
2 Think of a fact about the sport.
3 Share with the class. Who has the most interesting fact?

> **Reading strategy**
>
> Distinguish between fact and opinion in an article.

2 💡 Read and underline the facts about scuba diving. Then circle the writer's opinion.

On my last holiday, I tried scuba diving for the first time. It was awesome! In scuba diving, you can go really deep underwater because you breathe with an apparatus on your back called a scuba. Scuba diving gives me an amazing sense of freedom under the water. I felt like one of the fish! No wonder it's so popular – there are as many as 6 million active scuba divers worldwide!

3 🎧 2-28 Read *Extreme Limits*. Find one fact about extreme sports.

Reading 1

EXTREME LIMITS

Have you ever done extreme sports? These are activities and sports which involve danger. They often include high speeds, **plummeting** from a great height, physical exertion, or all three! White-water rafting, **skydiving**, **climbing**, and **scuba diving** are some examples of these sports.

It's hard to find exact numbers on the popularity of extreme sports, but statistics from various organisations confirm that they are becoming more popular. In the United States alone, over 3 million skydiving jumps are made yearly. An American company compiled a report on the top 111 physical activities in the country. The report said that from 2007 to 2014 the number of people climbing only grew by around 19,000 people. But from 2014 to 2015 it grew by almost 150,000. The proportion of women climbers is increasing too, up from 16% in 2002 to 36% now. Not all sports are growing: hang gliding isn't as popular now as it was in the 1990s. But **paragliding** and paramotoring (paragliding with a giant fan) are becoming more popular.

"You get a bit addicted to the feeling," says Agnes Danson, a paragliding instructor. "A good flight involves **ascending** higher, and **descending** in different, more acrobatic ways. It's the best feeling in the world! I'm so lucky to have it as my job!"

It's the start of a warm, clear day. Agnes gathers a group of amateur paragliders and explains what they're going to do. Among them are university friends Max Stone and Lisa Cox. "We finished our exams and I thought, 'Let's go and do something crazy,'" says Lisa. She's done skydiving before and found it terrifying. "I just remember thinking, 'Hold it together, hold it together.' I was desperate to be on the ground." She hopes this will be a bit calmer. Max, on the other hand, is very excited. He enjoys **mountain biking** and has competed in **triathlons**, but has never done anything up high. "I get bored so easily – extreme sports are so **energising**," he says.

Lisa is up first. Then the rest take off, and it's clear they're having fun. Smoothly, gracefully, they **glide** back and forth over the hillside. When required, the instructors make things more exciting with big swings and **spirals**. It's an impressive sight!

Nat O'Reilly is watching her dad, Spike, enjoy his 60th birthday present – his first ever skydive. He's never been before. "That was awesome," he says on landing. Nat has tried skydiving ("thrilling!"), bungee jumping ("incredible!") and scuba diving ("the worst bit was stepping off the boat backwards"). It didn't start an addiction like it does in others.

She talks about scuba diving in a casual manner – good, yes, not amazing, but no need to do it again. "It's trying new things, isn't it?" she says. "It can be scary, but have you ever regretted trying something new? I haven't."

Avoiding boredom is a common theme among people who do extreme sports. Studies say that extreme sports evolved as a reaction to an increasingly safe life. As daily life lacks risks, people feel the need to experience the thrill of risk-taking. Another reason for an increase in the popularity of extreme sports is modern technology. Technology in safety devices and sports equipment have made many sports safer than they used to be. Video clip websites have also spread the popularity of these activities.

Extreme sports are a huge craze today. The psychology behind their popularity seems to be that it's human nature to take risks for excitement. And as long as people seek adventure, extreme sports will continue to attract large numbers.

4 Do you enjoy taking risks? Why / Why not?

135

Comprehension 1

1 Read *Extreme Limits* again. Write facts and opinions about skydiving.

Fact: Skydiving is an extreme sport.

....

Opinion: ....

....

2 Who would say the following? Read and write *L* (Lisa), *M* (Max), *N* (Nat), or *S* (Spike).

1 "That was the best birthday present ever!" ....

2 "Skydiving was very scary. I hope I'll enjoy paragliding more." ....

3 "I've tried scuba diving before, but I'm not addicted to it like other people are." ....

4 "I play a lot of sports, but I've never jumped off anything until today." ....

3 💬 Role-play with a friend.

1 **Student A:** You're the reporter who wrote *Extreme Limits*. Interview Max after his paraglide jump.

Student B: You're Max from *Extreme Limits*. Answer the reporter's questions.

2 Swap roles. Choose another person from the article to interview.

Listening 1

4 💬 Which Olympic sports do you like watching and why? Discuss with a friend. Do you like the same sports?

Listening strategy

Distinguish between fact and opinion in a news report.

5 🎧 2-29 Listen. Which extreme sports are mentioned in the news report?

6 🎧 3-01 Listen again and complete. Then write *F* (fact) or *O* (opinion).

| closer | stuffy | urban |
| youthful | 46.1% | 48.8% |

1 People believe future Games will be more .... and more ....

2 A total of .... of the Tokyo 2020 athletes will be women. ....

3 .... of competitors at Rio 2016 were women. ....

4 The IOC is seen to have a .... image. ....

5 The speaker feels that the Olympic Games have become much .... to their vision. ....

136

Vocabulary 1

1 Find these words in *Extreme Limits*. Then write the words and add more examples.

> ascend   climbing   descend
> energizing   glide   mountain biking
> paragliding   plummet   scuba diving
> spiral   skydiving   triathlon

Extreme sports

Words to describe airborne sports

2 🎧 3-02 Listen and say.

🇬🇧 British	🇺🇸 American
energising	energizing

3 💬 Work with a friend. Imagine you're doing some extreme sports. Describe them to your friend. Use the words below.

> amazing   awesome   crazy   energizing   incredible   terrifying

I'm skydiving. It's so energizing to jump off a plane and plummet towards Earth!

Wow! I'm white-water rafting. It's …

4 ▶ 9-2 BBC Watch Part 1 of the story video. Does Yan like sports?

Grammar 1

1 🎬 9-3 BBC Watch Part 2 of the story video. Read and complete.

2 🎬 9-3 BBC Watch Part 2 of the story video again. Who's jealous of Yan?

I've .... met anyone like Yan.

.... he .... won a medal for chess?

3 Read the grammar box and complete.

> **Grammar**
>
> **Present Perfect**
>
> We use **Present Perfect** + *ever/never* to talk about experiences up to now.
> **Have** you **ever been** mountain biking?
> No, I**'ve never been** mountain biking.
>
> You can use **before** at the end of your question or answer.
> 1 **Have** you .... **been** bungee jumping **before**?
> 2 Yes, I**'ve been** bungee jumping ....

4 Read *Extreme Limits* again. Circle the sentences with *Present Perfect* + *ever/never*.

5 Read and circle.

1 **Have** / **Has** your brother ever **been** / **be** mountain biking?
2 I've **never** / **ever** tried base jumping before.
3 My sister has **gone** / **went** scuba diving in Australia **before** / **ever**.
4 Have you **never** / **ever** tried snowboarding before?

138

6 Look and complete.

1. Have you ever been _____ ?
   Yes, I _____ . It was great!

2. Have you _____ been _____ ?
   No, I _____ . But my brother has.

3. I've _____ been _____ before. I really want to go when I'm older.

4. _____ your sister been _____ ?
   Yes, she has. She goes every summer.

Speaking 1

7 Look at the questions below. Answer them for you. Write two more questions.

Have you ever …

1. been in a helicopter? _____
2. won a competition? _____
3. taken a big risk? _____
4. _____
5. _____

8 Look at your answers from Activity 7. Discuss in a group.

1. Ask and answer the questions.
2. Who in your group has done the most interesting things?

Have you ever been on a rollercoaster?

Yes, I have. I love them!

Me, too!

Speaking strategy

Explore where your experiences are similar or different from other people's.

139

Pre-reading 2

1 💬 Discuss with a friend.

1 Have you ever been to the theater?
2 Have you ever read a play?
3 Have you ever performed in a play?

> **Reading strategy**
>
> Explain the differences between plays and stories.

2 💡 Read. How can you tell this is a play and not a story?

Act 1, Scene 1

(Set in a school gym. ZOE, ELIAS, and SUE are standing in a group.)

ZOE: Have any of you seen Bruno today?

ELIAS: No, I haven't. He wasn't in P.E. class this morning.

(MS. DUKE runs into the gym. She's out of breath.)

SUE: Ms. Duke! Are you OK?

MS. DUKE: *(between gasps of air)* Children! Come, quick! It's Bruno! You have to see this!

---

3 🎧 3-03 Read *Come On, Grandpa!*. Look at Act 1, Scene 1, and underline the stage directions.

Reading 2

COME ON, GRANDPA!

Characters: Grandma (Maria), Isla, 8, Noah, 10, Mom (Eva), Doctor, Grandpa (Leonard Simms)

Act 1, Scene 1

(Grandpa lies in a hospital bed. Around him are GRANDMA, MOM, ISLA, NOAH, and the DOCTOR.)

DOCTOR: Well, Mr. Simms, you just have a small burn on your hand. It will heal by itself.

GRANDMA: What a relief!

GRANDPA: *(laughing)* That's the last time I try to make French fries!

DOCTOR: Actually, we ran some tests and they say you have very high **cholesterol**. It's essential that you **reduce** it. Otherwise, you're at high risk of a heart attack. You'd really benefit from exercise and a healthy diet.

GRANDMA: *(sadly)* Oh, no.

NOAH: Don't worry, Grandma – we'll help Grandpa get fit!

Scene 2

(A few weeks later. GRANDPA, ISLA, NOAH, and GRANDMA are sitting at the kitchen table.)

ISLA: You need to get fit, Grandpa. Do you like any sport?

GRANDPA: I love sport! I've never missed a game for the local soccer team.

140

NOAH: Grandpa! The **players** do all the work – you have a **relaxing** time on the sofa and watch them play!
GRANDMA: Come to **yoga** with me, Len.
GRANDPA: That's just sitting around, too!

(MOM enters carrying a mountain bike.)

MOM: We have a surprise for you, Dad!
GRANDPA: (almost speechless) A bike!
ISLA: Have you ever ridden a bike?
GRANDPA: Yes, I have.
ISLA: Did you like it, Grandpa?
GRANDPA: I loved it! They say you never forget.

Scene 3

(ISLA and NOAH are visiting GRANDMA and GRANDPA.)

NOAH: Hi, Grandma. Where's Grandpa? Has he gone out on his bike?
GRANDMA: No dear, he did that this morning. He's gone out for a run now with his running **partner**.
ISLA: Is he running as well now? Has he become a fitness **addict**?
GRANDMA: He's become a **member** of a running club. Here he is now.

(GRANDPA enters in a sweatsuit.)

ISLA: Grandpa, are you running and cycling now?
GRANDPA: Yes, I'm going to enter a duathlon next month.
NOAH: What's a duathlon?
GRANDPA: It's a **race** where you run and cycle; like a triathlon, but no swimming. I have my eyes on the **prize** in the over-60s **category**. I can't wait!
ISLA: That sounds great! Don't you want to swim as well?
GRANDMA: Isla! Don't go putting ideas in his head!

Scene 4

(ISLA, NOAH, MOM, and GRANDMA are waiting at the finish line of the duathlon, cheering. GRANDPA is approaching on his bike.)

NOAH: (cheering) Come on, Grandpa!!
MOM: Come on, Dad! You can do it!
GRANDMA: He's about to cross the line! I've never seen him move so fast!

(GRANDPA skids his bike and goes crashing to the ground. SCREEEEEECH! CRAAAASH!)

GRANDPA: Aaaargh!
ALL: Grandpa – are you OK?!

Act 2, Scene 1

(The family is back in the hospital. GRANDPA's not in the room. They are talking to the doctor.)

DOCTOR: Mr. Simms has broken his wrist and has a few cuts and bruises. He'll be absolutely fine – thanks to his fitness **program**, his heart is as strong as an ox!

(GRANDPA walks into the room with his arm in a sling – still wearing his mud-splattered clothes from the race and looking a bit bruised.)

ISLA: Grandpa!
NOAH: Guess what, Grandpa? You crossed the line before you fell – you've won the over-60s category!
GRANDPA: That's great! What's the prize?
ISLA: Free entry to the next duathlon!

(All laugh. GRANDMA rolls her eyes a little.)

4 Grandpa worked towards a goal. Think of when you have worked towards a goal. Discuss with a friend.

Comprehension 2

1 Read and answer the questions.

I couldn't believe that almost a year after Grandpa burned his hand we were in the hospital again! The doctor assured us that Grandpa was going to be fine and there was no problem with his heart. Just then, Grandpa walked into the room with his arm in a sling. "Guess what, Grandpa?" I said. "You crossed the line before you fell – you've won the over-60s category!"

1 Which scene of the play is this?

2 Which character's account is it?

3 How is this text different from the play?

2 Read *Come On, Grandpa!* again. Answer the questions by making inferences from the text.

1 How exactly did Grandpa burn his hand?

2 How did Grandpa enjoy sports before the doctor told him to exercise?

3 Do you think Grandma has a healthy lifestyle? Why / Why not?

4 How do you think Grandpa gets fit so fast?

5 How's the mood in the hospital different in Act 1, Scene 1 and Act 2, Scene 1?

3 Perform the play in groups.

1 Practice the play in groups of six.

2 Perform to the class. Act without the script if you can.

Listening 2

4 Do you enjoy exercising? What is your favorite kind of exercise to do? Discuss with a friend.

Listening strategy

Summarize the main points of an audio interview.

5 (3-04) Listen. Which character from the play is being interviewed?

6 (3-05) Listen to the interview again. Summarize the interview in three sentences. Then compare your summary with a friend.

Interview with Local Grandpa

One year ago, he burned his hand.

Vocabulary 2

1 Find these words in *Come On, Grandpa!*. Then write them next to their definitions. Write your own definitions for the remaining words.

addict	category	cholesterol	member
partner	player	prize	program	race
reduce	relaxing	yoga

1 .... : **(v)** a synonym for this word is *to lessen*
2 .... : **(n)** this means a person who can't stop doing something
3 .... : **(n)** in the context of exercise, this word means a schedule
4 .... : **(n)** a group of similar people or things
5 .... : **(n)** this word means an individual who belongs to a club
6 .... : ....
7 .... : ....
8 .... : ....
9 .... : ....
10 .... : ....
11 .... : ....
12 .... : ....

2 🎧 3-06 Listen, check your answers, and say.

3 💡 Read and complete the similes. Use the words from the box.

| a bat | a feather | an owl | the hills |

1 as light as ....
2 as blind as ....
3 as old as ....

4 💬 Discuss with a friend.

1 Are any of the similes in Activity 3 the same in your language? Which are different?
2 Translate some similes in your language to English.

Grammar 2

1 Watch Part 2 of the story video again. Has Mr. Thompson ever won an Olympic medal?

2 Read the grammar box and circle.

> **Grammar**
>
> **A** **Have** you **ever done** a bungee jump? Yes, I **have**.
> **B** Wow – what **was** it like? **Were** you terrified?
>
> 1 Sentence **A** / **B** refers to a specific event in the past.
> 2 Sentence **A** / **B** refers to an experience at any time before now.
>
> We can ask general questions about life experience in **Present Perfect**, and then follow up using **Past Simple**.

3 Read *Come On, Grandpa!* again. Circle an example of a Present Perfect question and a Past Simple follow-up.

4 Read and circle.

1 Have you ever been in a helicopter? **No, I didn't. / No, I haven't.**
2 Have you ever gone hiking before? **Yes, I have. / Yes, I did.**
3 When did you go? **I went last year. / I've been last year.**
4 Did you get tired? **No, I haven't. / No, I didn't.**
5 Have you ever tried bungee jumping? **No, I haven't. / Yes, I did.**

5 Read the interview. Write the questions in the correct tense.

UNDERWATER DIVER

We talked to underwater diving star Ellie Thomas about her amazing experiences!

1 INTERVIEWER: _____ ?

Ellie: Yes, I have been scuba diving before. Many times! I love being close to nature.

2 INTERVIEWER: _____ ?

Ellie: I started scuba diving when I was just 12 years old.

3 INTERVIEWER: _____ ?

Ellie: Yes, I was scared when I first went scuba diving. But I'm not anymore!

4 INTERVIEWER: _____ ?

Ellie: No, I haven't been free diving before. It's dangerous, and I can't hold my breath very long!

6 Complete the sentences. Use the correct form of the verbs in parentheses.

1 I've been to Paris. I _____ there last summer. (go)
2 I've _____ soy milk before. I didn't like it. (try)
3 I've _____ in a submarine. I saw a coral reef! (be)
4 I've won an art competition. I _____ a set of watercolor paints. (get)

Speaking 2

7 Turn the sentences into questions. Then ask and answer with a friend. If your friend says yes, ask three follow up questions.

I've run a race.
I've played in a sports team.
I've been on a boat.

I've sung karaoke.
I've tried an extreme sport.
I've been to another country.

Have you ever run a race?

Yes, I have.

Did you win?

Writing

1 Read Lara's blog post. Answer the questions.

1 What has she done a lot of times?
2 What did she just start doing?

As Cold as Ice!

Home | Blog
About

March 17th – My First Blog Post!

Hi, guys! I'm Lara. I've spent all my life in the mountains near a ski resort. My mom and dad are ski instructors. I can't remember a time when I didn't ski! I love the feeling when I speed down the mountain like the wind. When I'm on skis, I feel as free as a bird! I recently wanted a new challenge, so I've just started learning how to snowboard. I fell down a lot at first, but I got back up again. My instructor said I'm as cool as a cucumber! Snowboarding is amazing fun. You can do all sorts of jumps and tricks. My favorite jump involves rotating 360 degrees. When my mom saw me do it, she was very scared. She went as white as a sheet! I've just started racing professionally on skis as well. Now I can't decide whether I like skiing or snowboarding best!

2 Read the blog again and write down the similes.

1 ....
2 ....
3 ....
4 ....
5 ....

Writing strategy

Use similes to make your writing more exciting and expressive.
*The stars shone **like diamonds**.*

3 Work with a friend. What do the similes in Activity 2 mean?

4 Find a picture of one of your interests on the internet or in a magazine. Then go to the Workbook to do the writing activity.

146

Now I Know

1 Why do we play sports? Look back through Unit 9, remember what you learned, and write.

Lisa Cox: *She likes trying new things and new challenges.*

Nat O'Reilly: ....

Grandpa: ....

Ellie Thomas: ....

Lara: ....

My friends: ....

Me: ....

2 Choose a project.

Role-play an interview with a sportsperson.
1. Use the internet to research a sport.
2. Find out about someone who is famous for the sport.
3. Write an interview with them.
4. Role-play the interview with a friend.

or

Invent a new extreme sport.
1. Write the rules and the equipment you need.
2. Think of where people will play it.
3. Draw a picture of yourself playing the sport.
4. Present it to the class.

Self-assessment

Check (✔) or cross (✘) for you.

✘ I can't do this yet.   ✔ I can do this.   ✔✔ I liked doing this.

I can identify opinions.

I can understand the main points of an interview.

I can distinguish between fact and opinion.

I can indentify the key characteristics of texts.

I can talk about matters of personal interest.

I can describe past events, using descriptive language to add interest.

I can show similarity between two ideas.

10

What's causing extreme weather?

Listening
- I can identify specific information in spoken dialogs.

Reading
- I can recognize cause and effect relationships.
- I can guess the meaning of unknown words from the context.

Speaking
- I can take part in a discussion.

Writing
- I can create a new version of a familiar story.

1 Look at the picture and discuss.

1 What has happened here?
2 Why do you think this happened?
3 What problems will this cause?

2 Read and make notes. Then compare your answers with a friend.

1 What types of extreme weather do you know?
2 Where in the world can you find extreme weather?
3 Do you have any extreme weather events in your country?

3 10-1 BBC Look at the video still and predict. Is the man hot or cold?

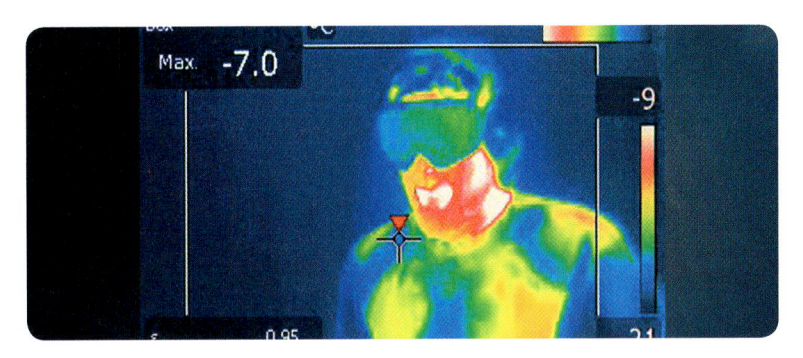

4 10-1 BBC Watch the video and check your answer from Activity 3. Then watch again and write T (true) or F (false).

1 The temperature of a freezer is -15 degrees.
2 You should wear only one layer of clothing in very cold weather.
3 *Wind chill* is when a thin layer of cool air is replaced by warm air.
4 Wind chill makes the temperature feel colder than it really is.
5 If your clothes are wet, you will get colder more quickly.

149

Pre-reading 1

1 💬 Think about the weather in your country. Discuss with a friend.

1. What's the weather like today in your country?
2. Is it normally like this at this time of year?
3. Has the weather in your country changed in recent years?

📖 Reading strategy

Describe the cause and effects of events in a text.

2 Read. What's causing the warmer summers?

Why are summers warmer than just a few years ago?
Martha Smithson, Liverpool

The answer's simple! Earth's climate is constantly changing. It's different today from what it was 100 years ago. Then, Earth was cooler than it is now. The average temperature in the year 1920 was 13 degrees Celsius, whereas today it is 16 degrees Celsius.

3 🎧 3-07 Read *Ask a Scientist!*. What's the difference between climate and weather?

Reading 1

Ask a Scientist!

Our expert scientist Yumi Tanaka is here to help answer your science questions. This week, 12-year-old Patricia asks Yumi about weather and climate.

I keep hearing about weather and climate. Are they the same thing?

Not quite. Weather is what you experience at a specific time. So, right now it's raining. Climate is the typical weather we can expect in a particular area. For example, the climate of Germany is mild. This means it's usually warm in summer and cool in winter. Weather can change from day to day, whereas climate takes a long time to change.

*If climate can take a long time to change, why do I keep hearing about **climate change**?*

Good question. Earth's climate is constantly changing and it always has been. In the past, Earth has been both warmer and cooler than now. Scientists have discovered that we're in a **period** of **global warming**. The planet's temperature has risen by about one degree Celsius in the past 100 years.

Only one degree? That's not much, is it?

No, but small changes in temperature can have very big effects. What's more, it's happened relatively quickly.

In the past, it's sometimes taken tens of thousands of years for the climate of the planet to change.

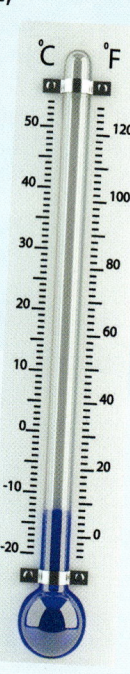

The North Pole

The South Pole

I see. Then why has it taken just 100 years this time?

Many scientists believe this is because of the actions of humankind. Temperatures started to increase in the middle of the 20th century – about the same time that we started to burn lots of fossil fuels, such as coal, oil and gas, to create electricity. When burning, fossil fuels produce carbon dioxide, nitrous oxide, and methane. These are called *greenhouse gases* and they trap heat in Earth's atmosphere.

That sounds like a problem for our planet, doesn't it?

Absolutely! Scientists believe greenhouse gases will cause temperatures to rise even further in the future, meaning extreme weather conditions will become more frequent.

Extreme weather? That sounds really bad, doesn't it?

It does, and it is. Extreme weather is a real problem. In fact, a recent study has suggested that by the end of this century as many as 152,000 people will die annually because of extreme weather. In 2010, that number was just 3,000.

That's terrible. What types of extreme weather are there?

In many parts of the world you can expect prolonged **heat waves** and **droughts**, when rivers dry out and crops fail. This will mean lots of people will die of hunger. It doesn't stop there. With the ice caps at the poles melting, you can expect to see many coastal areas disappear forever. And with the hotter weather, more water will **evaporate**, which will bring heavier rainfall and severe **flooding** to many areas.

So, heat waves, floods, drought, lots of rain ... any more types of disasters?

I'm afraid so. Do you know what **hurricanes** and **typhoons** are?

I think so. Are they storms with very strong winds that cause lots of damage?

Correct, hurricanes can **devastate** areas of North and Central America while typhoons affect countries in Asia. They'll become stronger and more frequent. The warmer temperatures will mean more water will evaporate and the warmer air will store this water, making rainfalls more **intense**.

Does that increase in temperature mean that winters won't be as cold?

I'm afraid not. You can also expect to see more extreme winter weather. There'll be more occasions of warm air meeting cold air, making **blizzards** and snowstorms more frequent. So, there'll be more storms all year round!

crops

ice caps

4 Do you think humans are to blame for global warming? Why / Why not?

151

Comprehension 1

1 Read *Ask a Scientist!* again. Read the causes and write the effects.

1 **Cause:** Snow and ice melting at the poles
   Effect: Increase in sea levels and coastal areas disappearing

2 **Cause:** Burning fossil fuels
   Effect: ....

3 **Cause:** Greenhouse gases in atmosphere
   Effect: ....

4 **Cause:** Increase in temperature
   Effect: ....

5 **Cause:** Heat waves and drought
   Effect: ....

6 **Cause:** More hurricanes and typhoons
   Effect: ....

2 Work in groups of four. Each choose one situation. Take turns explaining the effects.

1 Snow and ice at the poles are melting.
2 We are burning fossil fuels.
3 Temperatures are rising.
4 There are too many greenhouse gases in our atmosphere.

3 Discuss with a friend.

1 What's the climate of your country?
2 Are there any areas of your country that are in danger of severe flooding and rising sea levels?

Listening 1

4 Do you check the weather forecast before you leave the house? Discuss with a friend.

> **Listening strategy**
>
> Understand the main ideas in a radio weather forecast.

5 (3-08) Read about the hurricane and put the events in the order that they happened. Then listen and check.

a The hurricane makes its way inland. ☐
b Hurricane Harvey makes landfall. ☐
c Residents evacuate their homes. [1]
d Flooding occurs. ☐
e The intensity of the hurricane increases. ☐

6 (3-09) Listen to the news report again. What do the numbers refer to? Write.

| 56 | 4 | 130 | 100 |

1 Strength of the hurricane ....
2 Speed of the wind (kph) ....
3 Length of time since last hurricane of equal strength in years ....
4 Amount of rain expected (cm) ....

Vocabulary 1

1 Find these words in *Ask a Scientist!*. Then write them next to their definitions.

> blizzard   climate change   devastate
> drought   evaporate   flood
> global warming   heat wave
> hurricane   intense   period   typhoon

1 More water than usual on dry land. ....
2 To damage something very badly. ....
3 A severe snow storm with strong winds. ....
4 The increase in Earth's average temperature. ....
5 Low rainfall resulting in a shortage of water. ....
6 A tropical storm in Asia. ....
7 Strong, powerful, extreme. ....
8 A period of hot temperatures, warmer than usual. ....
9 A tropical storm in Central and North America. ....
10 Length or portion of time. ....
11 A permanent change in the Earth's weather conditions. ....
12 To change from a liquid into a gas. ....

2 Read and complete.

1 The heavy rain caused a .... in nearby villages.
2 The very strong winds that hit Tokyo are called a ....
3 The .... is causing a .... , and the land is too dry for drops to grow.
4 This blizzard is so .... !

3 Work in pairs. Explain the difference between the words.

1 hurricane and typhoon
2 blizzard and heat wave
3 intense and devastate
4 flood and drought

4 Ask and answer with a friend.

1 How is a hurricane different from a regular storm?
2 How can we prevent global warming?

153

Grammar 1

1 🎬 10-2 [BBC] Watch Part 1 of the story video. Read and complete.

Look at my gloves. They're nice, ... ?

🇬🇧 British	🇺🇸 American
sledge	sled

2 🎬 10-2 [BBC] Watch Part 1 of the story video again. Who saves Oli?

3 Read the grammar box and circle.

> **Grammar**
> **Question tags**
>
> Joe can't swim, **can he?** You like snow, **don't you?**
>
> 1 If the first part of the sentence is positive, the question tag is **positive / negative**.
> 2 If the first part of the sentence is negative, the question tag is **positive / negative**.
> 3 We use the same auxiliary in the question tag as in the first part of the sentence. When there's no auxiliary, we use *do* or *did*.

4 Read *Ask a Scientist!* again. Circle sentences with question tags.

5 Read and match.

1 It's Monday today,   a does she?
2 You like pasta,   b isn't it?
3 You aren't cold,   c can we?
4 We can't swim,   d are you?
5 James and Evie are late again,   e aren't they?
6 Maria doesn't eat meat,   f don't you?

6 Look and write.

1 They aren't playing tennis, *are they*?

2 He doesn't like fish, _____?

3 It's going to rain, _____?

4 I can't play well, _____?

Speaking 1

7 Listen and repeat.
3-10

Your name's Petra, isn't it?

It isn't cold today, is it?

8 Complete the sentences about a friend.

1 Your name's _____, _____?
2 You don't live in _____, _____?
3 You like _____, _____?
4 You don't like _____, _____?
5 You can't _____, _____?
6 You're _____, _____?

9 Work with a friend. Look at Activity 8 and ask and answer. Remember to use the correct intonation.

You like dancing, don't you?

Yes, I do.

Why?

Because it keeps me fit.

155

Pre-reading 2

1 💬 Discuss with a friend.

1. In which countries does it snow a lot?
2. What kinds of activities can you do in the snow?
3. Can snow ever be dangerous?

> **Reading strategy**
>
> Determine the meaning of unknown words from the context in a text.

2 💡 Read and answer. Do you think the word *rush* describes a fast or a slow speed?

I was swimming in the ocean when I felt a few drops of rain on my head. I looked at the beach and saw Dad waving at me, so I swam back to shore. "A bad storm is coming," he said. "We have to get back to our hotel." We packed up our things and rushed back to the hotel. Luckily, it wasn't far from the shore. The rain was coming down a lot stronger now.

3 🎧 💬 The title of the story is *Trapped!*. Where do you think the family was trapped? Discuss with a friend. Then read and check your answer.

Reading 2

Trapped!

Marta opened her eyes. She was too excited to sleep any longer. She peered out of the log cabin window into the morning. The snowy mountain was sparkling in the morning sunshine. Today was the final day of Marta's winter vacation with her family in the mountains. It had been a perfect trip so far.

"Wake up, everybody. We have to make the most of our last day here!" she called. Her parents rubbed their eyes and **stumbled** out of bed. After a big breakfast, the family put on their ski clothes and stepped out into the harsh cold. "We need to get more food and firewood at the supermarket," said Dad. "Should we go now?"

"No way!" said Marta. The **ski slopes** are too busy if you get there after 9 a.m.! Let's **ski** now!"

"OK, OK," laughed Dad, "we'll go later." They made their way to the ski **resort**, and Marta used her **sled** to get quickly down the hill.

At the resort, the family put on their skis and took the **chairlift** up to the ski slopes. Marta zoomed past people skiing, **snowboarding**, and sledding. She was a **gifted** skier, and had been skiing since she was four years old. As they enjoyed their morning, snow started falling. "That's strange," said Mom to herself.

Outside, the blizzard was getting worse, and the wind was howling around the little cabin. The snow was getting deeper, and was now covering the windows. It seemed like the storm would never stop.

After four hours, the wind died down and the snow stopped. The blizzard was finally over. Dad tried to open the door, but it wouldn't budge. "We're trapped," he said. "The snow must be almost two meters high! It looks as if we'll be here for a while."
"I'm sure we'll be rescued," Mom said to Marta, who looked worried. Marta smiled, and the family eventually fell asleep.

BANG! BANG! BANG! Marta opened her eyes. "What was that noise?" she asked sleepily. It was still dark. Surely it must be morning now? The noise was coming from the front door. Dad tiptoed over and opened the door. Light poured into the cabin. Three members of the mountain rescue team were standing there. They had dug a **path** through the snow. "How are you all? We've been working all night to rescue people **stranded** on the mountain." "Thank you. You saved us!" cheered Dad. Marta and Mom beamed with happiness.

As they were leaving, Marta suddenly stopped. "One moment," she said. "There's something I have to do." She rolled a **snowball** that was bigger than herself and then rolled a second, smaller one. With the help of the mountain rescue team, she lifted it onto the larger snowball. "Look, it's no ordinary snowman … it's a blizzardman!"

After lunch, the snow began to fall more heavily and the wind whipped across the ski resort. The temperature suddenly plummeted rapidly. It was now below freezing. "Let's go back to the cabin. I don't like the look of this weather," said Dad, shivering with cold. "If we don't get back soon, we're in trouble."

Once inside the cabin, Mom tried her cell phone: no signal. "What are we going to do?" she asked. "I'll try the radio," Marta answered. She turned the dial on the battery-operated radio until she found a newsflash. "… We have reports of a sudden and severe blizzard in the mountains. People are advised to stay indoors until the emergency is over. All **power lines** in the area have collapsed, and electricity supplies have been cut off …"

"We didn't get any food or firewood!" gasped Marta. "I'm sorry, we should have gone to the store before skiing."
"It's OK," said Mom. "The weather forecast said there wouldn't be any snow today. It's not your fault."

The hours went by and the family huddled together in the darkness.

4 How important is it to be prepared for extreme weather? Why?

Comprehension 2

1 Find these words in *Trapped!*. Check (✓) the picture that best describes each word.

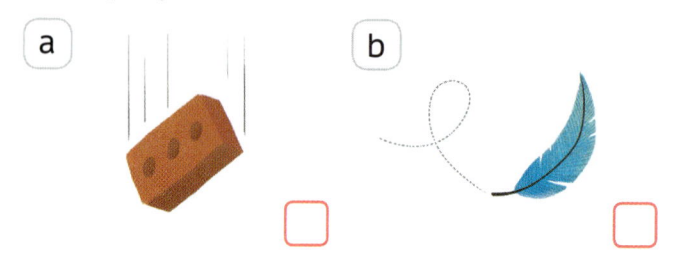

1 zoom
a   b

2 rapidly
a   b

3 huddle
a   b

2 Find these words in *Trapped!*. Write the words next to their meanings.

> beam   budge   howl
> shiver   tiptoe

1 to smile widely ....
2 to walk on your toes ....
3 to move ....
4 to shake due to the cold ....
5 to make a loud, high noise ....

3 Discuss with a friend.

1 Why do you think Marta was so excited?
2 Why wasn't there any food or fuel?
3 Why couldn't Dad open the door?

Listening 2

4 Storm chasers are people who want to be present during a bad storm. Do you think it is dangerous to do this? Discuss with a friend.

🎧 Listening strategy
Listen for meaning and definitions of words.

5 🎧 3-12 Listen to the interview with Melissa, a storm chaser. What does she think of amateur storm chasers?

6 🎧 3-13 Listen again. Write definitions for the words.

1 thrill ....
2 meteorology ....
3 to safeguard ....

7 💡 Would you like to be a storm chaser? Why / Why not?

Vocabulary 2

1 Find these words in *Trapped!*. What part of speech are they in the story? Write *N* (noun), *V* (verb), or *A* (adjective).

1. chairlift ....
2. gifted ....
3. path ....
4. power lines ....
5. resort ....
6. skiing ....
7. ski slope ....
8. sled ....
9. snowball ....
10. snowboard ....
11. stranded ....
12. stumble ....

2 Work in pairs. Write definitions for the words in Activity 1.

3 Swap your definitions with another pair. Can you guess the words?

4 Read and write for you.

1. Is it possible to go skiing in your country? ....
2. Have you ever been on a chairlift? ....
3. Have you ever been in a blizzard? ....
4. What's the difference between sledding and snowboarding? ....
5. Is there anything that your friend is gifted at? ....

5 Work in groups of three or four. Create a story using the words from Activity 1. Then perform your story to the class.

Grammar 2

1 ▶ 10-3 BBC Watch Part 2 of the story video. Read and complete.

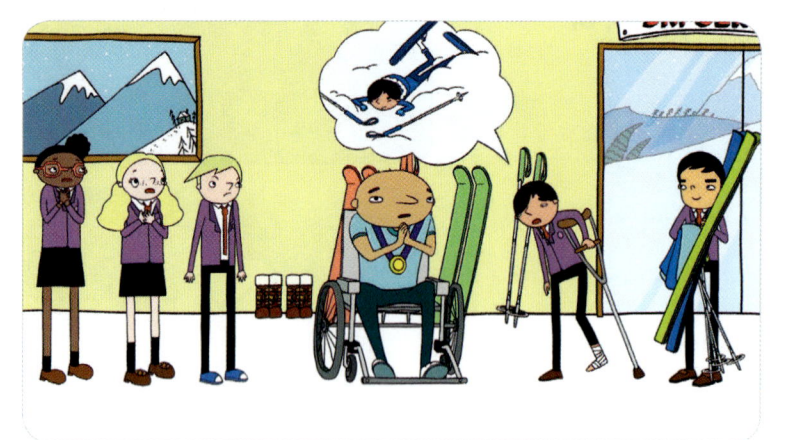

If Oli's leg gets .... ,
he can ....
But if it .... get better,
we .... another act!

2 ▶ 10-3 BBC Watch Part 2 of the story video again. Who did Oli and Yan go to see?

3 Read the grammar box. Circle Present Simple verbs in the sentences.

> **Grammar**
>
> **Zero conditional**
>
> **If** you **heat** water, it **evaporates**.
>
> We use the **zero conditional** to talk about general truths.
>
> If I 'm bored, I usually listen to music.
>
> My mom gets angry if I come home late.

4 Read *Trapped!* again. Circle sentences with the zero conditional.

5 Read and circle.

1 If it **'s** / **was** raining, I always take an umbrella.
2 If I **study** / **will study** hard, I pass my exams.
3 Jamie **gets** / **get** angry if he **wasn't eat** / **doesn't eat**.
4 If she **ridden** / **rides** her bicycle to school, she **felt** / **feels** tired.
5 If the wind **reaches** / **reach** 56 kilometers per hour and it **'ll be** / **'s** snowing, it's called a blizzard.

6 Look at Activity 5. What word can replace *if*?

7 What happens in the following situations? Write using the zero conditional.

1 If you flip a light switch, _____ .
2 _____ , the grass gets wet.
3 Ice melts if _____ .
4 If you mix red and blue paints, _____ .
5 _____ , you get burned.
6 If you heat water, _____ .

Speaking 2

8 Complete the sentences with things that are true for you. Then write two more sentences.

If I miss the school bus, _____ .
If I don't eat breakfast, _____ .
If I don't do my homework, _____ .
If it's sunny outside, _____ .
If my friend is sad, _____ .
If _____ .
If _____ .

Speaking strategy

Express agreement or disagreement politely.

9 Share your answers from Activity 8 with a friend.

> If my friend is sad, I buy them ice cream.

> Do you? I don't. I go to the movie theater with them.

Writing

1 Read *The Wind and the Sun*. What's the message of the story?

The Wind and the Sun

The Wind and the Sun were having an argument about who was strongest. The Sun saw a traveler walking down the road and said, "I know how we can settle this argument. Whoever can make that traveler take off his coat is the strongest. You first."

The Sun hid behind a cloud, and the Wind went first. He began to blow as hard as he could, trying to blow off the traveler's coat. But the harder he blew, the more tightly the traveler wrapped his coat around his body. Soon, the Wind was out of breath and had to give up. Then the Sun came out and shone as brightly as possible. The traveler soon took off his coat in the extreme heat.

2 Read *The Blizzard and the Heat Wave*. How are the stories in Activities 1 and 2 similar and how are they different?

The Blizzard and the Heat Wave

The Blizzard and the Heat Wave were arguing about who could cause the most damage. The Heat Wave saw a city in the distance and said, "I know how we can decide our dispute. Whoever can cause people to evacuate the city is the winner. You begin."

The Blizzard went first. She began to snow as heavily as she could, while blowing a strong wind. Suddenly the city streets were white. But they were also empty, as everyone went inside their homes to keep warm. Soon, the Blizzard was exhausted and stopped. Then the Heat Wave came out. He made the sun shine strongly and the temperatures rise. Everybody soon left their homes, got into their cars, and drove to the beach, where they enjoyed a day in the sun.

3 **WB 141** Think about a short story that you like. Then go to the Workbook to do the writing activity.

Writing strategy

Change details in a familiar story by replacing them with your own ideas.
*Little **Green** Riding Hood went to see her **grandfather** ...*

Now I Know

1 What's causing extreme weather? Look back through Unit 10, remember what you learned, and write.

Earth's climate is constantly changing.

....

....

2 Choose a project.

Create a poster about climate change in your country.

1. Think about how climate change is affecting the weather in your country.
2. Plan and design your poster.
3. Create the material that you need for your poster.
4. Present your poster to the class.

or

Write a news report about a recent extreme weather event.

1. Think of a recent extreme weather event.
2. Think about where and when the event happened and what the details were.
3. Write a news report.
4. Role-play as a TV presenter and present your report to the class.

Self-assessment

Check (✔) or cross (✘) for you.

- ✘ I can't do this yet.
- ✔ I can do this.
- ✔✔ I liked doing this.

I can identify specific information in spoken dialogs.

I can recognize cause and effect relationships.

I can guess the meaning of unknown words from the context.

I can take part in a discussion.

I can create a new version of a familiar story.

11

Why do we cook?

Listening
- I can extract key details from extended monologs.
- I can understand the main points in extended factual talks.

Reading
- I can understand key details in fiction and non-fiction texts.
- I can infer information.

Speaking
- I can take part in a discussion.
- I can talk about matters of personal interest.

Writing
- I can describe the steps in a process.

1 Look at the picture and discuss.

1 What's this person doing?
2 Does it look difficult?
3 Do you think she likes her job?
4 Would you like to do this job?

2 Read and make notes. Then compare your answers with a friend.

1 What's your favorite food to eat?
2 Do you know how it's made?
3 Do you ever cook?

3 11-1 BBC Look at the video still and predict. How's Professor Mark Post hoping to stop hunger around the world?

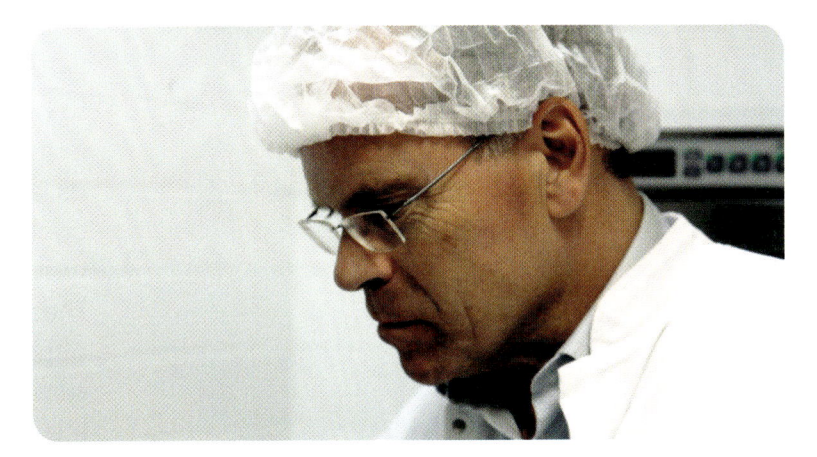

4 11-1 BBC Watch the video and check your answer from Activity 3. Then watch again and answer the questions.

1 How much lab-grown beef could be made from one cow?
2 Why doesn't lab-grown beef look like traditional muscle tissue?
3 Why is salt added to the muscle fibers?
4 What meat does the lab-grown beef taste like?

Pre-reading 1

1 A lot of the food that we eat is cooked. What are the benefits of cooking food? Discuss with a friend.

> **Reading strategy**
>
> Identify the reasons given for why something happens.

2 Read. Why can you find restaurants from all around the world on a British Main Street?

Walk down the Main Street of any town or city in the U.K., and you will see restaurants from all around the world. This is because the British love food from many different countries. Italian restaurants came top in a 2017 survey of favorite restaurants in the U.K., with Indian restaurants a close second. Traditional British food was only third on the list.

3 Read *What's Cooking?*. How does cooking food make it safer to eat?

Reading 1

What's Cooking?

Sue King

Food hygienist Sue King tells us how cooking food keeps us safe ... and how it made us what we are today.

The food we eat every day has often been cooked. But why is this? And did you know that cooking demonstrates that humans have come a long way over the past 200,000 years?

Let's get one thing straight. Not all food needs to be cooked. Salad vegetables, such as lettuce and cucumber, are normally eaten raw, as is fruit. Even some foods that we usually cook can be eaten raw. I'm thinking about fish that we eat as sushi, like tuna and salmon. These are all safe to eat without being cooked, although these are the exceptions. We make sure the majority of what we eat has been in the oven, the **frying pan**, or the **saucepan** before eating it.

oven

Let's discuss the main reason for cooking food. Bacteria, such as salmonella, E. coli, and campylobacter, which are all found in raw or undercooked meat, can make you seriously sick. About 600 million people worldwide get food poisoning every year from eating food contaminated with bacteria. Thankfully, cooking food kills bacteria. This means our burgers and steaks are safe to eat.

You also need to be careful when preparing raw meat. Clean the **chopping board** that you used for **dicing** your beef, wash your hands, and don't use the same knife to **chop** vegetables. If you don't clean everything, bacteria can hang around and contaminate other food.

But that's not the only reason we cook food. We boil pasta, **bake** bread, **steam** broccoli, **grill** corn, and **fry** eggs. Some foods need to be cooked to make them **edible**. Some foods taste better cooked. And it's also easier to **digest** cooked food because cooking breaks down the fibers in the food. If you put a piece of meat on the barbecue, it soon becomes tender. So, when we chew it, it breaks down quickly and we can digest it easily.

Also, cooking helps to release proteins in food. Proteins are nutrients, just like carbohydrates and vitamins, and are essential in a balanced diet. They help to grow our muscles and they keep us feeling full for longer. This means you stop wanting **snacks** between meals.

It also means we're less likely to become overweight. If we eat the same food raw, we cannot access these proteins.

This leads us on to how cooking has helped us to evolve as a species. Professor Richard Wrangham, a scientist from Harvard University, suggests humans are what we are simply because we learned to prepare food properly.

Why is this? We all know that our bodies need calories – which is simply energy – to function, and the source of our energy comes from food. About a quarter of the calories we eat are used by the brain; the rest are used by our muscles. So, eating helps us to think and move around. Remember that we digest cooked food more easily than raw food? Well, our bodies also find it easier to extract calories from cooked food than the raw equivalent. Homo habilis, early humans who ate little more than raw meat, would have had difficulty digesting food and obtaining all the calories they needed.

The next species of human, Homo erectus, learned to control fire and it was here that mankind started to cook food. Professor Wrangham believes this allowed humans to evolve bigger brains and smaller stomachs because we could get more calories from food and digest it more easily. Homo erectus became the dominant species and Homo habilis soon became extinct. Humans continued to evolve (and cook!) until we reached the species that we are today – Homo sapiens.

4 If humans had never learned to cook, do you think we would still be living like other wild animals?

Comprehension 1

1 Read *What's Cooking?* again. What are some reasons why humans cook food?

1 ....
2 ....
3 ....
4 ....
5 ....

2 Discuss with a friend.

What's the reason why …

1 cooking helps us digest food?
2 you shouldn't use the same knife to chop meat and then vegetables?
3 Homo erectus was more successful than Homo habilis?

3 What other precautions do we need to take to make sure our food is safe to eat? Discuss with a friend.

Listening 1

4 How can you make sure you don't get sick from the food you eat? Discuss with a friend.

> **Listening strategy**
>
> Extract the key details from an extended monolog.

5 🎧 3-15 Listen. Can you tell if food is properly cooked just by looking at it?

6 🎧 3-16 Listen again. Complete the sentences in your own words.

1 A food scientist lets people know ....
2 Many people believe that you can tell if food is bad by smelling or ....
3 A good way of checking that food is cooked is to ....
4 Food poisoning doesn't come ....
5 Washing your hands is ....

7 Read. Which statements are true and which are false? Why? Discuss as a class.

1 The taste and smell of food will tell you if it's bad.
2 Once you've cooked food, you can leave it uncovered for hours.
3 Food poisoning can affect you months after you've eaten something bad.
4 Preventing food poisoning is easy.

8 Have you ever cooked outside? Discuss with a friend.

Vocabulary 1

1 Find these words in *What's Cooking?*. Then write them next to their definitions. Write your own definitions for the remaining words.

| bake | chop | chopping board | dice | digest | edible |
| fry | frying pan | grill | saucepan | snack | steam |

1 .... : **(n)** This is something that you eat between meals.
2 .... : **(n)** This is a deep, metal container that you use for cooking.
3 .... : **(v)** This means to cook over a direct heat, like on a barbecue.
4 .... : **(v)** This is when you cook food with oil on the stove.
5 .... : **(n)** You chop vegetables on this.
6 .... : **(n)** This is a round, metal container with a long handle that you use for cooking food with oil.
7 .... : ....
8 .... : ....
9 .... : ....
10 .... : ....
11 .... : ....
12 .... : ....

2 🎧 3-17 Listen, check your answers, and say.

3 Circle the odd one out.

1 bake / steam / fry / cut
2 frying pan / snack / saucepan / chopping board
3 edible / cook / chop / bake
4 dice / chop / cook / frying pan

4 💬 Work with a friend. Choose one food and take turns describing ways that you can prepare it. Use the words from Activity 1.

> You can fry an egg in a frying pan.

> You can also boil an egg in a saucepan.

169

Grammar 1

1 Watch Part 1 of the story video. Read and complete.

Jade wants to .... for the Arts Show after school.

2 Watch Part 1 of the story video again. What did Jade's mom bring her to eat?

3 Read the grammar box. What do you notice about the second verb in each sentence?

> **Grammar**
>
> **Verb + *to* + infinitive**
>
> He **agreed to help** his mom prepare the food.
> Sara **wants to be** a chef when she's older.
> Todd **refused to tell** anyone the secret ingredient.

4 Read *What's Cooking?* again. Circle sentences with verb + *to* + infinitive.

5 Read and match.

1 I booked a cabin and I can't wait
2 My mom says I have
3 The bakery had
4 I can't believe my friends plan
5 Kyung-hee's dog tried

a to take a bite of Tom's sandwich!
b to go to the park without me.
c to go snowboarding with my family next month.
d to finish my homework before dinner.
e to close early because they ran out of bread.

6 Complete the sentences. Use *to* + the infinitives from the box.

do   eat   help   read   share

1 Jack wanted .... pizza every single day.
2 He refused .... his homework last night.
3 I've promised .... Dad tidy the backyard.
4 Marta, Anna, and Maria will agree .... the reward money.
5 She hopes .... a lot of books this summer.

Speaking 1

7 Write five sentences about you. Use the verbs from the box and *to* + infinitive.

> **Speaking strategy**
> Show interest when giving and asking for personal views and opinions.

agree   hope   promise   refuse   want

1 ....
2 ....
3 ....
4 ....
5 ....

8 Look at Activity 7. Read your sentences to the class. Answer any questions.

I want to study music in college when I'm older.

Oh, that's interesting. Why do you want to study music?

Because I want to be a violinist when I'm grown up.

171

Pre-reading 2

1 Read. Do you agree with the quote? Discuss with a friend.

> "When a man's stomach is full, it makes no difference whether he is rich or poor."
> *Euripides*

Reading strategy

Compare and contrast similar traditional stories from two different cultures.

2 Read how the stories of *Tom Thumb* and *Thumbelina* begin. What are the similarities and differences?

Tom Thumb

A farmer and his wife wanted a son, but they couldn't have children. They were given a wish and they wished for a son. He was very small, so they called him Tom Thumb.

Thumbelina

A woman wanted a daughter, but she couldn't have children. She was given a wish and she wished for a daughter. She was very small, so she called her Thumbelina.

3 Read *Stone Soup* and *Axe Soup*. Why do you think the villagers in both stories are unhappy?

Reading 2

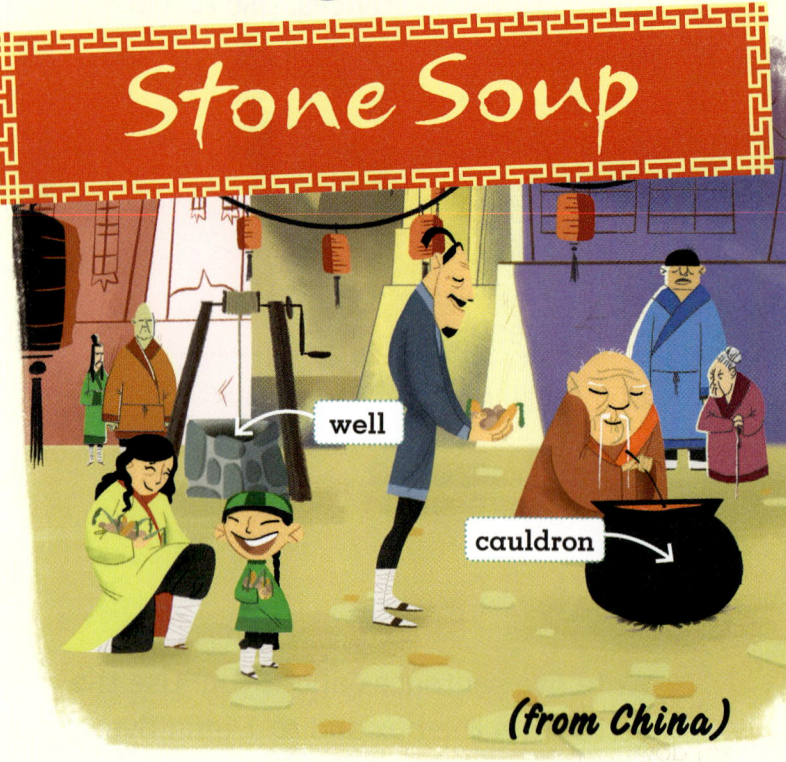

Stone Soup

(from China)

There was once a wise man who travelled the country to discover what made people happy. One day he arrived at a village where everyone was working on their own piece of land. They spent so much time working that they didn't even talk to each other.

When the wise man entered the village, nobody welcomed him. The villagers ignored him and continued working.

"This is an unhappy village, so I'll cheer it up with a bit of stone soup," he said. He went to the village square and made a small fire. He filled a cauldron with water from a nearby well, which he put on the fire to boil.

A young girl was observing him. "What are you doing?" she asked.

"I'm making stone soup … but I need a stone," he replied. "Can you bring me one?"

The girl soon returned, struggling with a massive stone, which the wise man put into the cauldron.

An old man came by and demanded to know what was happening. "We're making stone soup, but we need a **bunch** of green onions and some carrots for a crunchy **texture**," answered the wise man.

"What did he say?" asked the old man. "He asked if we could get green onions and carrots for his soup," said his wife. Off they went to get some **organic** vegetables from their garden. Next came the village police officer, who soon went home to get some noodles. One by one, the villagers asked what was going on … and one by one they returned home to get different **ingredients** for the soup. After a while, the wise man tasted the soup. "It's ready, but we need something to serve it in." The villagers went home to fetch bowls.

When they returned, the wise man poured some soup into each. He said, "Please sit and enjoy your **meal**. And please have conversations with each other." The villagers sat down, ate their soup, and talked to their neighbours. Never again was the village an unhappy place.

AXE SOUP
(from Russia)

- bowl
- axe
- kindling

There once was a woodcutter who went around the country chopping down trees for people. One freezing cold day, he was starving and needed to eat. However, he didn't have any money to buy anything. He entered a village that looked poor. He knocked on the door of one house and an elderly man answered.

"Could you give me a little food?" asked the woodcutter.

"I've got nothing. We're all very hungry and nobody has got any food, but the rich lady in the mansion might give you something," the old man said.

The woodcutter knocked on the door of the big, expensive mansion. The rich lady answered and the smell of bread greeted the woodcutter. "Please can I have some food?" he begged.

"No," she shouted before quickly slamming the door in his face.

The woodcutter saw an old cauldron in the village square, so he made a fire and filled the cauldron with water from a nearby well. When the water was bubbling, the woodcutter put in his axe. The rich lady approached and asked what he was doing.

"I'm making axe soup," he responded. "It's delicious, but I **require** salt and pepper. Bring me some and you can try the soup when it's ready." The rich lady went to get some salt and pepper and when she returned, the woodcutter added the **condiments** and smelled his soup. "It's very good. What I need to make it tastier is garlic and celery. Make sure it's fresh, nothing **rotten**." Off she went, soon to return. The woodcutter added the vegetables and **mixed** the soup. "That's delicious. Now it needs some lamb." When she returned, the woodcutter added the **raw** meat to the cauldron and tasted the axe soup. "That's the best axe soup I've ever made, but it's missing one vital ingredient."

"What's that?" asked the rich lady.

"Everybody in the village. Go and get them. There are enough **servings** for us all." Eager to try the soup, the rich lady knocked on everybody's door and invited them to the **feast**.

4 On what occasions do you eat meals with other people in your country? What kind of food do you eat?

Comprehension 2

1 Work with a friend. One student writes similarities between *Stone Soup* and *Axe Soup*. One student writes differences. Then discuss.

Similarities

....

....

....

Differences

....

....

....

2 Can you think of two other stories that are similar, like *Stone Soup* and *Axe Soup*? In what ways are they similar and different to each other?

3 Work with a different friend. Ask and answer for *Stone Soup*. Then swap roles and ask and answer for *Axe Soup*.

1 Why did the main character go to the village?
2 Why did the main character want to make people happy?
3 How did the main character check that the soup was ready?
4 What do you think happened after everybody shared the soup?

Listening 2

4 Do you know anyone who has tried a special diet? Why did they do it? Did it work? Discuss with a friend.

Listening strategy
Guess the meaning of unknown words in a dialog.

5 🎧 3-19 Listen. Whose brother ate only raw food? Check (✓).

Beth's ☐   Joseph's ☐   James's ☐
Maddy's ☐   The teacher's ☐

6 🎧 3-20 Listen again. Check (✓) the topics that are mentioned.

1 most popular food in the class ☐
2 different diets ☐
3 dishes containing vegetables ☐
4 what a vegetarian is ☐

7 Write the definitions.

1 vegetarian ....
2 vegan ....
3 fruitarian ....

8 The man doesn't recommend eating only raw fruit, nuts, and seeds. Why do you think that is? Discuss.

Vocabulary 2

1 Find these words in *Stone Soup* and *Axe Soup*. What part of speech are they in the stories? Write *N* (noun), *V* (verb), or *A* (adjective).

1 bunch ....
2 condiment ....
3 feast ....
4 ingredient ....
5 meal ....
6 mix ....
7 organic ....
8 raw ....
9 require ....
10 rotten ....
11 serving ....
12 texture ....

2 Work in pairs. Write definitions for the words from Activity 1.

3 Swap your definitions with another pair. Can you guess the words?

4 Complete the sentences with your own ideas.

1 I like to eat raw .... and ....
2 My family has a big feast at ....
3 My favorite condiment to eat with food is ....
4 At home, I like to eat boiled ....
5 I like foods with a .... texture.

5 Work in groups. Describe your favorite foods using the words from Activity 1.

175

Grammar 2

1 ▶ 11-3 BBC Watch Part 2 of the story video. What did the doctor tell Oli to do? Read and complete.

The doctor told Oli ....

2 ▶ 11-3 BBC Watch Part 2 of the story video again. What does Yan use to eat his meal at school?

3 Read the grammar box and complete.

> **Grammar**
>
> **tell** and **ask** in reported speech
>
> "Be quiet!"
> The teacher **told** the class **to be** quiet.
>
> "Where can I get a drink?"
> She **asked** me where she **could** get a drink.
>
> When reporting an order we use **tell** with **to** + **infinitive**. When reporting a question we use **ask** with **to** + **infinitive** or **ask** with a **wh- question** and the past form.
>
> 1 "Wash the dishes!"
>   Mom told me .... the dishes.
> 2 "Where's the printer?"
>   He asked me where the printer ....

4 Read *Stone Soup and Axe Soup* again. Circle an example of reported speech.

5 Read and circle.

1 "Go to your room!"
   He told her **to go** / **to went** to her room.

2 "Where's the theater?"
   He asked where the theater **was** / **is**.

3 "What are you doing?"
   She asked me what I **am doing** / **was doing**.

4 "Can you help us?"
   They asked me **to help** / **helping** them.

5 "Put your phones away before the movie starts."
   The announcer **told** / **tells** us to put our phones away.

6 Complete the reported speech. Use the correct form of the verb.

1 **Dad:** "Can you make me a cup of tea?"
Dad asked me *to make him a cup of tea* _____ .

2 **Teacher:** "Maria, be quiet!"
The teacher _____ .

3 **Joe:** "What's your favorite food, Dan?"
Joe _____ .

4 **You:** "Pass me a pencil, please."
You _____ .

5 **Me:** "What do you want to do this weekend, Anna?"
I _____ .

7 Work in pairs. Read the text messages. Then take turns reporting the orders and questions.

1 Jake, meet me at the park at 7 o'clock. Tim

2 Anna, when can you clean up your bedroom? Love, Mom

3 Hi Ollie, what do you want to do on Saturday? David

4 Marta, call me when you can. Sara

Speaking 2

8 Answer the questions for you.

1 What's your favorite fruit? _____
2 What did you do last night?
_____
3 What movies do you like?
_____
4 What do you normally do on the weekend? _____

9 Work in pairs. Ask and answer the questions from Activity 8. Then repeat the questions in reported speech.

What's your favorite fruit?

Beth asked me what my favorite fruit was.

177

Writing

1 Read the recipe. Answer the questions.

1 About how long does it take to make this dish?
2 What is this dish served with?

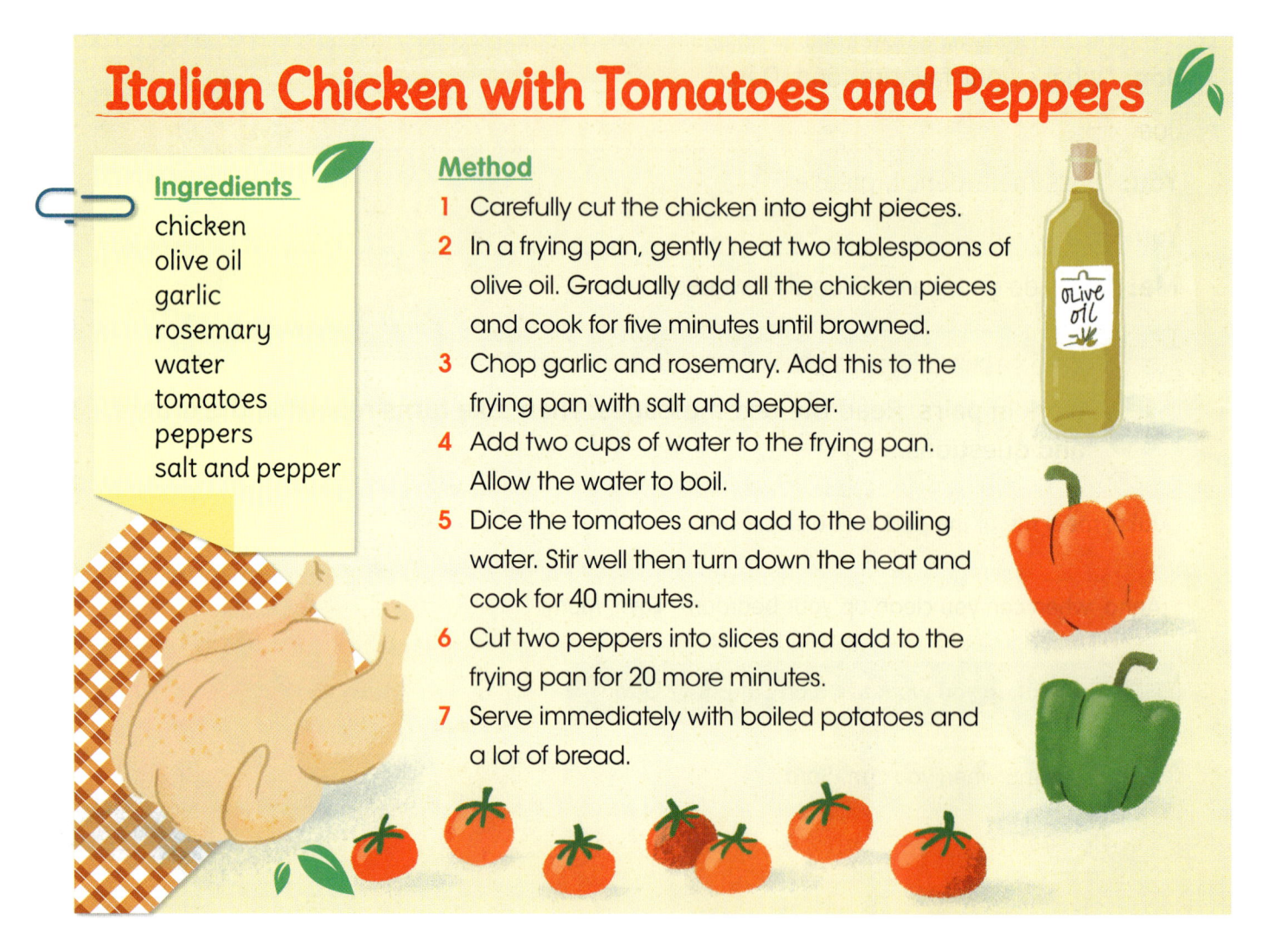

Italian Chicken with Tomatoes and Peppers

Ingredients
chicken
olive oil
garlic
rosemary
water
tomatoes
peppers
salt and pepper

Method
1 Carefully cut the chicken into eight pieces.
2 In a frying pan, gently heat two tablespoons of olive oil. Gradually add all the chicken pieces and cook for five minutes until browned.
3 Chop garlic and rosemary. Add this to the frying pan with salt and pepper.
4 Add two cups of water to the frying pan. Allow the water to boil.
5 Dice the tomatoes and add to the boiling water. Stir well then turn down the heat and cook for 40 minutes.
6 Cut two peppers into slices and add to the frying pan for 20 more minutes.
7 Serve immediately with boiled potatoes and a lot of bread.

2 Read the recipe again. List the words that tell us how to perform an action.

1 *carefully*
2 ....
3 ....
4 ....
5 ....

Writing strategy

Use words to describe in detail how a task needs to be completed.
Carefully cut the potatoes into cubes.

3 WB 155
Think about your favorite meal. Find the recipe for it from a book or the internet. Then go to the Workbook to do the writing activity.

178

Now I Know

1 Why do we cook? Look back through Unit 11, remember what you learned, and write.

....

....

....

2 Choose a project.

Create a poster about food hygiene.

1 Think about the hygienic ways that we prepare and cook food.
2 Plan and design your poster.
3 Create the material that you need for your poster.
4 Present your poster to the class.

or

Make a world recipe book.

1 Work as a class. Each choose a dish from a different country.
2 Research the ingredients and how the dish is made.
3 Write a recipe with pictures.
4 Collect all the recipes together and make a world recipe book.

Self-assessment

Check (✔) or cross (✘) for you.

✘ I can't do this yet.   ✔ I can do this.   ✔✔ I liked doing this.

I can extract key details from extended monologs.

I can understand the main points in extended factual talks.

I can understand key details in fiction and non-fiction texts.

I can infer information.

I can take part in a discussion.

I can talk about matters of personal interest.

I can describe the steps in a process.

12
How do we learn?

Listening
- I can identify specific information in spoken dialogs.
- I can extract key details from extended monologs.

Reading
- I can identify the writer's overall purpose.
- I can identify evidence that supports the writer's point of view.

Speaking
- I can make suggestions.
- I can talk about matters of personal interest.

Writing
- I can signal direct speech.

1 💬 **Look at the picture and discuss.**

1. What are the students doing?
2. Which subject are they studying?
3. Do you think they're learning something interesting?

2 💬 **Read and make notes. Then compare your answers with a friend.**

1. What do you like most about learning new things?
2. Are you good at remembering things?

3 ▶️ 12-1 BBC **Look at the video still and predict. What will computers be able to do in the year 2029?**

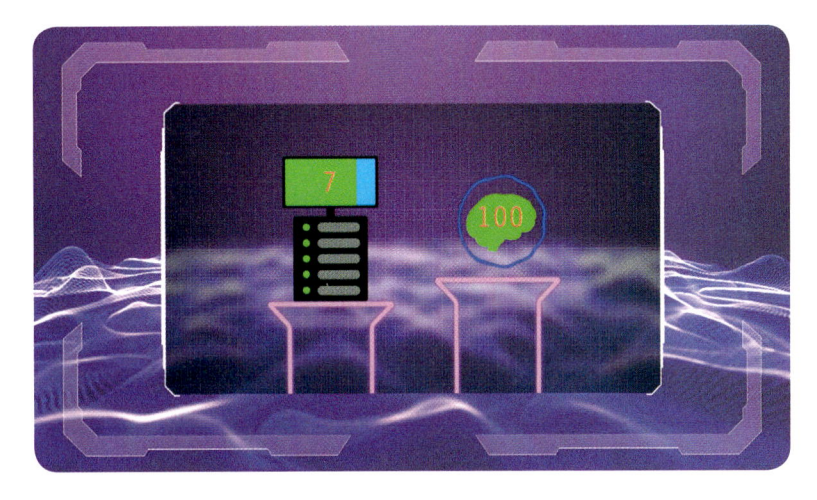

4 ▶️ 12-1 BBC **Watch the video and check your answer from Activity 3. Then watch again and answer the questions.**

1. What could 16,000 computers recognize after watching 10 million YouTube videos?
2. What was the name of the computer that was successful on U.S. TV?
3. Why was the computer able to be successful on TV?

181

Pre-reading 1

1 💬 Discuss with a friend.

1. Do you ever read poems?
2. Do you have a favorite poem?
3. Can you recite a poem that you have learned by heart?

> **Reading strategy**
>
> Explain the main differences between poems and stories.

2 💡 Read. How does the poet feel when asked a question in class? How do you know?

When Teacher Asks Me a Question

When teacher asks me a question,
My stomach ties in knots.
My hands get sweaty, my heart beats fast
And my face feels far too hot.
My mouth gets dry as a desert;
There's a ringing in my ears.
Speaking out loud in the classroom
Is my very biggest fear.
I close my eyes and take a breath,
I know that I can do this.
I count to 10 and then I speak:
"Yes, I'm here today, Miss!"

---

3 🎧 3-21 Read *A Surprising Test* and *The Day of the Exam*. Which is a short story and which is a poem? Why do you think the authors chose these different writing styles?

Reading 1

A Surprising Test

"Let the test begin," said Mr Honeyburn. Mr Honeyburn is our Maths teacher and he's obsessed with numbers. We learned our multiplication tables every class through **rote repetition**. I imagine him doing **calculus** while eating his cornflakes and insisting that his sandwiches are **symmetrical**.

Today, the school inspector was visiting, and to make things worse, we had a surprise test … and I hadn't **revised** or **prepared** at all. No time to **study** now. My palms were sweating; butterflies were dancing in my stomach. I needed air. "Please, Mr Honeyburn, can I open the window?" I asked. "Yes, Pupil Six, you can." Mr Honeyburn called us by numbers because he couldn't remember our names.

I opened the window, but before I could sit down, a HUGE gust of wind sucked all the test papers out the window. They tossed and turned around the playground and Mr Honeyburn cried, "Pupils One to Nine, chase the nine papers heading east-westerly. You're all facing south, how many degrees clockwise will you have to turn to face the right direction? That's Maths problem number one."

Without pausing, he hollered, "All remaining odd numbers chase the five papers heading towards the pond, which is 100 metres away. If you run at an average speed of 10 kilometres per hour, and the papers are travelling at approximately seven kilometres per hour, how long will it take you to retrieve them? That's maths problem number two."

He continued, "All remaining numbers proceed towards the big tree. I can see eight papers at a height of five metres. How high will the tallest pupil in your group need to climb to reach them? That's number three!"

We went about our tasks until there were no papers left. At that moment, the door burst open. In marched the school inspector. She was as tall as a giraffe and pencil thin. She was an official-looking woman, wearing a smart black suit. She peered over her clipboard. Her beady little eyes stared at us; she looked around the classroom, and then stood still.

She stayed in that frightening position for five seconds before she exclaimed, "That was the best Maths lesson EVER. I never knew that a Maths lesson could be so creative!" A wave of relief swept across the room. Mr Honeyburn fainted – we **estimated** for about three seconds!

The Day of the Exam

I'm sweating and my knees are shaking,
The pen in my hand is jiggling and quaking.

Here we're sitting in the old exam hall,
I so wish I was out in the golden fall.

The test now begins, heads go down.
This is far too difficult, I worry and frown.

The exam paper is laughing, telling me I'll fail.
I just want to go home, I silently wail.

My mind wanders back to the **research** I did.
That pile of books on my floor, under which I hid.

I read and read and read some more.
Taking notes every day was such a chore.

"If I **set goals** for myself, I'll do well in the test."
That's what I thought, but I'm still feeling stressed.

Wait one moment, look here and see.
A question I know, the answer is C.

And here is another, now I'm feeling smart.
All these answers, I know them **by heart**.

Where on Earth can you find Timbuktu?
Which country's capital is Mogadishu?

How many oceans and seas can you name?
The exam is so easy, it's just like a game.

The bell then goes, put down your pens.
I'm so happy the exam has come to an end.

One week later, grades come out today.
It's an A for me, hip hip hooray!

4 Why do you think the inspector liked Mr. Honeyburn's class so much?

Comprehension 1

1 Read *A Surprising Test* and *The Day of the Exam* again. Then answer.

1 How are the two readings different?
....

2 How are they similar?
....

3 What effect does the rhyming in the poem have on you as a reader?
....

4 Which do you think would be easier to learn by heart? Why?
....

2 Read and answer the questions.

1 How were Pupil Six and the author of the poem feeling before their exam?

2 How were they feeling after their exam?

3 Did Pupil Six study for the test?

4 Which subject is being tested in *The Day of the Exam*?

3 Find these words and expressions in *A Surprising Test*.

1 a phrase that means you're very nervous
....

2 a synonym for shout

3 a difficult or boring task

4 a simile to describe a tall person

5 a way to say *very thin*

6 an adjective to describe small, round eyes

Listening 1

4 Do you have special study techniques for doing well at school? Discuss with a friend.

Listening strategy

Recognize when a listener is checking their understanding.

5 (3-22) Listen. Which sentences does the interviewer use to check understanding? Check (✓).

1 So ... ☐
2 Do you mean ... ? ☐
3 If I understand correctly ... ☐
4 This is ... isn't it? ☐

6 (3-23) Who uses each of the following study techniques? Write names.

1 Does past papers.
2 Takes a lot of notes.
3 Reads notes ten times.

7 Think of an exam where you did very well or very badly. Why do you think this was? Discuss with a friend.

184

Vocabulary 1

1 Find these words in *A Surprising Test* and *The Day of the Exam*. What does each word mean? Then complete the chart.

by heart ☐   estimate ☐   repetition ☐   revise ☐   set goals ☐   symmetrical ☐
calculus ☐   prepare ☐   research ☐   rote ☐   study ☐   take notes ☐

Ways to study	Math words

2 Look at Activity 1. Think of the meaning of the words. How did you figure them out? Number the techniques you used.

1 I already knew the word.
2 It's similar to a word in my own language.
3 I used the words around it.
4 I used a dictionary.

3 Look at the words. Write *N* (noun), *V* (verb), or *A* (adjective). Add another form of each as indicated.

1 estimate   V   →   estimation   (n)
2 prepare   →   (n)
3 symmetry   →   (adj)
4 repetition   →   (v)
5 revise   →   (n)

4 Choose six words from Activity 1. Write sentences for each word in your notebook. Then compare with a friend.

185

Grammar 1

1 Watch Part 1 of the story video. Answer the questions.

1 Which exam did Jade do the best in?
....
2 Why did she do well in this exam?
....
3 Which exams did she do the worst in?
....

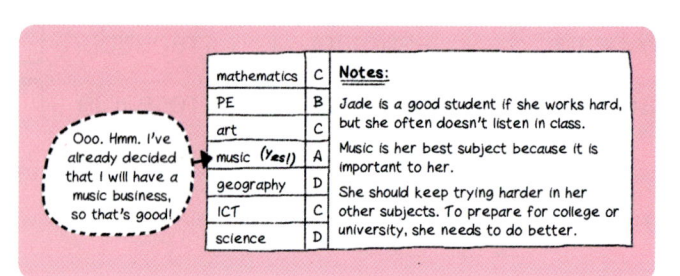

		Notes:
mathematics	C	Jade is a good student if she works hard, but she often doesn't listen in class. Music is her best subject because it is important to her. She should keep trying harder in her other subjects. To prepare for college or university, she needs to do better.
PE	B	
art	C	
music (Yes!)	A	
geography	D	
ICT	C	
science	D	

Ooo. Hmm. I've already decided that I will have a music business, so that's good!

2 Read the grammar box and complete the sentences.

Grammar

First conditional

We use the **first conditional** to talk about the likely results of a future action.

If Jade **studies** more in science and geography, she**'ll pass** the exams.

The *if* part doesn't have to appear at the start of the sentence.

1 .... I pass the exam, I'll be happy.
2 I'll be happy .... I pass the exam.

3 Read *A Surprising Test* and *The Day of the Exam* again. Circle sentences with the first conditional.

4 Read and match.

1 If he passes all of his exams,	a play video games all day.
2 If it's raining tomorrow, I'll	b stop shouting, I'll tell her to be quiet.
3 I'll be really happy if	c his parents will take him to a restaurant.
4 His parents will be sad if	d he stops going to ballet classes.
5 If I don't	e get at least a B on this test, I'll be upset.
6 If she doesn't	f I'm chosen for the school play.

5 Look at the first half of the sentences in Activity 4. Think of new endings to the sentences. Then compare with a friend.

6 💬 Play the *First Conditional Chain Game*.

If it's sunny tomorrow, I'll go to the beach.

If I go to the beach, I'll swim in the ocean.

If I swim in the ocean, I'll catch a fish.

Speaking 1

7 Read the requests. Think of what you would offer for each. Write first conditional sentences.

- Help me with my math homework.
- Give me some chocolate.
- Play soccer with me.
- Help me study for my exam.
- Buy me a pizza.
- Go to the shopping mall with me.
- Ride the bus with me.

1 If you help me with my math homework, I'll lend you my favorite video game.
2 ....
3 ....
4 ....
5 ....
6 ....
7 ....

8 💬 Work in pairs. Look at Activity 7 and read aloud the requests and your offers. Check (✓) the offers that your friend agrees to.

9 💬 Tell the class about your requests and offers.

Jorge will help me with my math homework if I lend him my favorite video game.

Pre-reading 2

1 How good are you at remembering these things? Discuss with a friend.

1. new words in English
2. important dates
3. people's names
4. homework

> **Reading strategy**
>
> Refer to details when making inferences from a text.

2 Read. Does the author think that there are three learning styles? How do you know?

Learning Styles

Different people learn in different ways – that's nothing new! However, over the years learning styles have been cut down to three: visual, physical (kinesthetic), or audible. In fact, we could probably split each of these styles down even more. Learning experts have done just that and come up with seven styles.

3 Read *Memory Tips from the Masters*. Does the author think that improving memory skills is important in everyday life? How do you know?

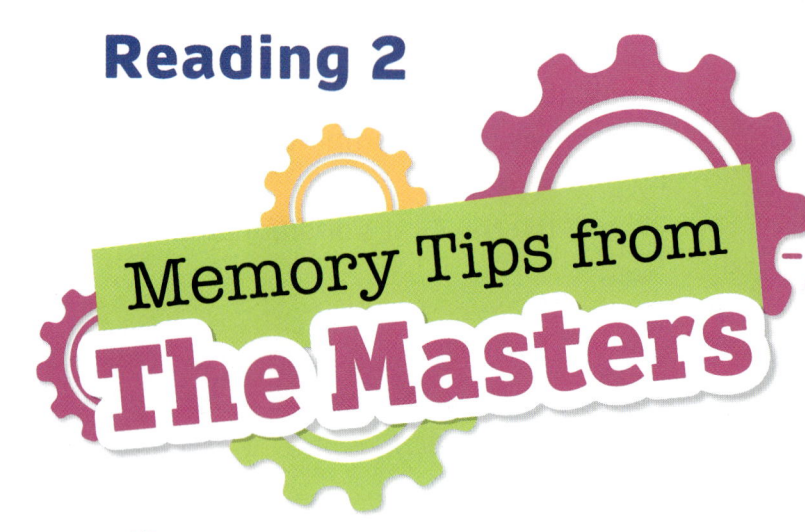

Reading 2

Memory Tips from The Masters

1 Memory Boot Camp

Here's a little secret: the people who perform amazing feats like **memorizing** the order of a deck of cards or hundreds of **random** numbers in minutes don't have photographic memories. They have normal brains like you and me. This past weekend I competed in the **annual** USA Memory Championship. It's a competition where **mental athletes** test their power of **recall**. Luckily for me, I learned a few tricks before I went.

My memory "boot camp" for this event started two weeks before the competition. I received a T-shirt and a training **manual**. There was also a list of the events, which included memorizing 117 names and faces in 15 minutes, memorizing 500 numbers in five minutes, and memorizing the order of a deck of cards. I knew it was going to be tough.

2 Memorable Memory Techniques

Do you know that there are two basic steps for all memory **challenges**? You can use them whether you're in a memory competition or just trying to remember where you left your bike.

> 1 Turn things that the brain can find difficult to remember, like names and numbers, into something different.
>
> 2 Find a place to store or *anchor* mental images where you're more likely to remember them.

For example, during the competition, one of the people I had to remember was called Dora and she was wearing a pair of sunglasses. First, I thought of Dora the Explorer. Then I drew a lot of little Dora the Explorers on her sunglasses in my **mind** to help me remember her name. I also had to remember a girl named Laurie. There was a girl called Lauren at school who always had a cold. I imagined a tissue box underneath Laurie's nose. It's quite an **abstract** image, but it was very memorable. I got those two names right, at least!

3 The Strongest System

For recalling lots of numbers and random cards, I knew that the same basic **techniques** still apply. However, stronger **systems** are also needed. When I had to remember 25 rows of 20 random numbers in five minutes, I nearly fell off my chair!

The technique everyone uses is the Dominic System, invented by memory champion Dominic O'Brien. In this system, each number from zero to nine has a letter. 15 is the letters A and E, for example. These letters are used as the initials of someone's name. So, 15 becomes Albert Einstein. You would then imagine Albert Einstein doing something like writing on a blackboard. Each number becomes a person and an action.

Then you need to find a familiar place to anchor the information. Memory champions build a *memory palace* to put the information in familiar places. It can be a made-up place or somewhere real: my memory palace is my house. For everyday use, the memory palace is a helpful **stimulus** for remembering a list of things. To do this, start a journey in your mind beginning at a familiar place. If you use your home as your memory palace, start at the front door. For a shopping list, imagine a carton of milk knocking on your front door. When you get inside, perhaps rice attacks you in your hall. Continue to your living room to find pretzels dancing on your rug.

If you don't think you're a visual person, use other senses like sounds, smells, or touch. Paying more attention to how things sound and feel can help your visualization skills. Start looking more at things and paying more attention. I'm still not a memory champion (I finished 40th out of 46), but at least now I'll remember your name if we're introduced!

4 Do you think you would do well at the Memory Championship?

Comprehension 2

1 Read *Memory Tips from the Masters* again. How do you think the author felt before, during, and after the Memory Championship?

2 Read the sentences and write **T** (true) or **F** (false). Then read and check.

1 The author had to remember 117 names and faces in 15 minutes. ....
2 There are three basic steps for all memory challenges. ....
3 To remember numbers, people use the Michael System. ....
4 The author had to remember 25 rows of 20 random numbers. ....
5 Memory champions build *memory planets* to store information. ....

3 Discuss as a class.

1 Why do you think some people find it easier to remember visual things rather than names and numbers?
2 How do you think the memory techniques from the article can help you at school?

4 Work in groups of three. Play a memory game.

1 Write down 10 random numbers between zero and nine.
2 Swap with another group. You have two minutes to memorize the numbers.
3 Turn your paper over. Can your group remember them all?

Listening 2

5 Do you have any special techniques for memorizing things? Discuss with a friend.

> **Listening strategy**
>
> Extract key details from extended informational monologs.

6 🎧 3-25 Listen. What three types of mnemonic does the speaker mention?

7 🎧 3-26 Listen again and answer.

1 What are the colors of the rainbow?
2 Which months of the year have 30 days?
3 When did Hawaii and Alaska become U.S. states?

8 Work in groups of three. Create a rhyme, name, or spelling mnemonic for these things. Then compare with other groups.

1 The order of the planets from the sun (Mercury, Venus, Earth, Mars, Jupiter, Saturn, Uranus, Neptune).
2 The oceans of the world (Atlantic, Arctic, Indian, Pacific, Southern).
3 To remember the spelling of the word *mnemonic*.

Vocabulary 2

1 Find these words in *Memory Tips From the Masters*. Then match the words to their definitions.

1 **abstract** (adj)
2 **annual** (adj)
3 **challenge** (n)
4 **manual** (n)
5 **memorize** (v)
6 **mental** (adj)
7 **mind** (n)
8 **random** (adj)
9 **recall** (v)
10 **stimulus** (n)
11 **system** (n)
12 **technique** (n)

a to remember something
b involving the mind
c without a plan or pattern
d based on ideas, not real things
e to learn something so you can remember it
f your thoughts and ability to think
g something difficult that needs skill
h a book that tells you how to do something
i a thing that makes something happen
j a way of organizing something
k a special way of doing something
l happening every year

2 Compare your answers from Activity 1 with a friend. Then cover the definitions, taking turns to remember them.

3 Listen. Write the missing word in each sentence.
3-27

1 Check the computer _manual_ if you have a problem.
2 Pick a _____ number below 10 and I'll guess what it is.
3 George _____ the day that he started school.
4 I learned a new _____ in my taekwondo class.
5 Intelligence and beauty are _____ concepts.
6 A good way to study is to _____ a lot of information.

4 Read and think. Then discuss as a class.

1 What challenges are there when you're learning new information?
2 In what situations do you find yourself unable to remember something?

191

Grammar 2

1 Watch Part 2 of the story video. Do we know how Emily did her magic trick? Then read and circle.

I **knew** / **know** he's good at tennis.

2 Read the grammar box and circle the parts of the sentence after *know (that)*.

> **Grammar**
>
> *know (that)*
>
> I **know that** Mogadishu is the capital of Somalia.
>
> After the verb **know (that)**, we use clauses, such as **he's married** or **broccoli is good for you**. They can act as sentences by themselves.
>
> 1 We know Canada is in North America.
> 2 She didn't know that his birthday was today.
> 3 Does he know we won the race?

3 Read *Memory Tips from the Masters* again. Circle the sentence with *know (that)*.

4 Read and complete. Use *know*, *that*, or both.

1 I _____ you're busy at the moment.
2 We know _____ you have to leave early tomorrow.
3 My parents _____ _____ I need new glasses.
4 I didn't _____ that you like pineapple on pizza!
5 I _____ _____ you went to Spain last year.

> **know + wh- word**
>
> We can use *know* + *wh-* words to say things we know about.
> I **know how** to write code.
> I **don't know when** the restaurant opens.

5 💬 Complete the sentences with your own ideas. Then compare with a friend.

1 Do you know how _____ ?
2 My mom doesn't know where _____ .
3 Only my best friend knows _____ .
4 My teacher knows _____ .
5 My friend's pet cat _____ .
6 I don't know _____ .

Speaking 2

6 Read. Check (✓) or cross (✗) for you.

> 💬 **Speaking strategy**
>
> Find out more about a friend by asking questions.

The Abilities Questionnaire!

I can speak Chinese. ☐	I can speak English. ☐
I can play a musical instrument. ☐	I can draw very well. ☐
I can swim. ☐	I can stand on my head. ☐
I can play basketball. ☐	I can understand calculus. ☐
I can sing well. ☐	I can cook. ☐
I can _____ ☐	I can _____ ☐

7 💬 Work in pairs. Discuss your answers from Activity 6. Ask questions to find out more information. Then tell the class about your friend's abilities.

- I know how to speak Chinese.
- Do you? When did you learn to speak Chinese?
- I knew that Maya can speak English, but I didn't know that she can speak Chinese.

Writing

1 Read. Where would you expect to find a text like this?

THE SCHOOL BELL

Teacher Profile: Ms. Nazari

Ms. Nazari has been principal of Smithdown High for an incredible 11 years. She's very popular with the students and teachers. Andre Carter, aged 12, says, "Ms. Nazari is awesome! She's the friendliest person in the school." History teacher Mrs. Almeida told us, "Sabina's warm smile helps us get through tough days!"

School Stories

Everyone at school has a story to tell about Ms. Nazari. Our favorite is when a soccer referee hurt his knee and Ms. Nazari ran onto the pitch to take over from him. Who knew she was a qualified soccer referee?

So, was Ms. Nazari a star student at school? Apparently not! She told us, "I was always chatting to my friends in class instead of listening to the teacher. I always tell students never to behave like I did as a child!" Well, it seems like there's hope for us all!

2 Read again and answer the questions.

1. Who is the article about?
2. Is she popular with students and teachers? How do you know?
3. What advice does she give to the students? Why?

3 What other articles would you expect to find in a school magazine? Work with a friend and write down three ideas.

1. ....
2. ....
3. ....

Writing strategy

Include direct quotes in an article for a school magazine.
"I've never had so much fun," laughed Sunita.

4 **WB 169** Choose a person to write about for the school magazine. Then go to the Workbook to do the writing activity.

Now I Know

1 How do we learn? Look back through Unit 12, remember what you learned, and write.

....

....

....

2 Choose a project.

Create a memory challenge.

1. Choose a memory challenge.
2. If necessary, do some research.
3. Prepare your memory challenge, writing it down if you need to remember.
4. Give your memory challenge to a friend or ask the class to compete against each other.

or

Make an exam preparation mind map.

1. Get a piece of paper and draw a circle in the middle of it.
2. Write "exam preparation techniques" in the center circle.
3. Think of the different ways that you can prepare for exams.
4. Complete your mind map.
5. Present your mind map to the class.

Self-assessment

Check (✔) or cross (✘) for you.

✘ I can't do this yet.   ✔ I can do this.   ✔✔ I liked doing this.

I can identify specific information in spoken dialogs.

I can extract key details from extended monologs.

I can identify the writer's overall purpose.

I can identify evidence that supports the writer's point of view.

I can make suggestions.

I can talk about matters of personal interest.

I can signal direct speech.

Dictionary

Unit 1

Key vocabulary

Artificial Intelligence *n* use of computer technology to make computers think and make decisions like humans
auto part *n* the different pieces of a car that are manufactured separately and used to build or repair cars
basic *adj* simple but important and necessary
blade *n* the flat cutting part of the knife, tool, or weapon
button *n* a small round object on a piece of clothing, that you push through a hole to fasten it
complicated *adj* having a lot of different parts, and difficult to understand or deal with
courageous *adj* the quality of being brave
develop *v* to change into something bigger, better, or more important
electronic *adj* used for making electronic, equipment such as computers and television
explode *v* to burst into small pieces with a loud noise and a lot of force
heat *v* to make something warm or hot
hologram *n* a special type of photograph or image made with a laser in which the objects shown look solid, as if they are real, rather than flat
human *n* a person
kitchenware *n* plates, bowls, knives, forks, spoons, etc. used in the kitchen
mechanical *adj* relating to machines
melt *v* if something solid melts, or if you melt it, it changes to a liquid when it becomes warmer
microwave oven *n* a type of machine that cooks food very quickly
risky *adj* if an action is risky, something bad might happen when you do it
radar *n* a system that uses radio waves to find out where ships and planes are, or the equipment used to do this
rotate *v* to go around like a wheel
screen *n* the flat glass part of the television or a computer
soggy *adj* too wet and soft
wheel *n* one of the round things under a car, bicycle, etc., that turns and makes it move
wiring *n* all the electrical wires in a building or machine

Unit 2

Key vocabulary

adventure *n* the exciting thing you do when new things happen to you
analyze *v* to examine something carefully in order to understand it or to find out what it contains
ancestor *n* a member of your family who lived a long time before you were born
ancient *adj* thousands of years old
artifact *n* an object, such as a tool or weapon, that was made a long time ago and is historically important
bone *n* one of the hard, white parts inside your body that form the structure of your body
buried *adj* placed or hidden underground
chamber *n* a room used for a special or official purpose
civilization *n* a society that is well organized and developed
clay *n* sticky soil that is used for making pots or bricks
entrance *n* a door, gate, or other opening that you go through to enter a place
excavate *v* to remove earth that is covering very old objects buried in the ground in order to discover things about the past
exit *n* a door that you can go through to get out of a place
fossil *n* a rock that shows part of an animal or plant that lived thousands or millions of years ago
frieze *adj* a narrow piece of decoration along a wall, either inside a room or on the outside of a building just under the roof
labor *v* to work hard
looter *n* someone who steals things
noble *n* important people in a high social class
occupy *v* if something occupies you or your time, you are busy doing it
precious stones *phrase* a rare and valuable jewel, such as a diamond
remains *n* the parts of something that are left after the rest is gone
settlement *n* a group of houses and buildings where people live
site *n* a place where something important or interesting happened
spot *v* to find

Unit 3

Key vocabulary

baggage *n* the cases and bags that you carry when you are traveling
belongings *n* the things that you own, especially the one you carry with you, for example coats, pens, or books
benefit *v* to get an advantage from something or to be helped in some way
border *n* the line between two states or countries
citizen *n* someone who lives in a particular town, state, or country and has legal rights there
economic *adj* relating to business, industry, and money in a country or area
employment *n* work that you do to earn money
environmental *adj* relating to the natural world, including water, air, land, and plants
essential *adj* important and necessary
fall apart *v* to break into pieces

immigrant *n* someone who comes to live in a country
increase *v* to have more of something
integrate *v* to become part of a group or society and be accepted by them
join *v* to become a member of an organization, society, or group
move abroad *phrase* to leave your country and going to live somewhere else
natural disaster *n* a natural event, such as a flood, earthquake, or tsunami, that kills or injures a lot of people
political *adj* relating to the government or politics of a country
ranch *n* a large farm with cows, horses, or sheep
refugee *n* someone who has to leave his or her own country because it is dangerous to be there
reunite *v* to bring people together again after they have been separated
settled *adj* feeling comfortable and at home
society *n* all the people who live in a country and the way they live
stranger *n* someone you do not know
wake *n* when friends and family get together when someone dies

Unit 4

Key vocabulary

advice *n* ideas that other people tell you, that help you decide what you should do
ambulance *n* a special vehicle for taking sick or injured people to the hospital
ankle *n* the joint between your foot and your leg
burn *v* to destroy or damage something with fire
complain *v* to say that you are annoyed about something or not happy with something
elbow *n* the joint where your arms bend
emergency *n* a very serious and dangerous situation that you must deal with immediately
fall over *v* to accidentally drop down onto the ground
fire alarm *n* a piece of equipment that makes a loud sound noise to warn people of a fire in a building
fire truck *n* a large vehicle that carries people and equipment to stop fires
first-aid kit *n* a box containing equipment needed to give immediate medical help in an emergency
follow *v* to move along behind someone else
grow *v* to get bigger in size or amount
happen *v* when something happens, there is an event that no one planned or expected
heroic *adj* very determined or brave
hurry *v* to do something or go somewhere quickly
injury *n* physical damage to someone's body
lie *v* something that you say which you know is not true
lie down *v* to be or move into a position in which your body is flat on something
paramedic *n* someone whose job is to help sick or injured people until they get to a hospital

police car *n* an official car used by the police
prank *n* a joke in which you play a trick on someone in order to make him or her look silly
severe *adj* very bad or serious
suddenly *adv* if something happens suddenly, it happens quickly, when you are not expecting it

Unit 5

Key vocabulary

African wild dog *n* a spotted dog of Africa
Amur leopard *n* the rarest big cat on the planet and critically endangered
balance *n* something equal in importance or effect to something that has the opposite effect
biodiversity *n* existence of a wide variety of plant and animal species living in their natural environment
bumblebee *n* a large bee
captivity *n* if a person or animal is in captivity, they are kept somewhere and are not free
chemical *n* a substance used in chemistry, or used for doing things, such as cleaning
ecosystem *n* the environment and all the plants and animals in a place, that are all connected with each other and have an effect on each other
entire *adj* all of something
environment *n* the natural world
flavorless *adj* flavorless food is uninteresting because it does not taste strongly of anything
mammal *n* an animal that drinks its mother's milk when it is young, for example a cow, lion, or person
missing *adj* something that is missing is not in the correct place and you cannot find it
nature *n* the world and everything in it not controlled by humans
pangolin *n* a scaly mammal found in tropical Africa, South Asia, and Indonesia
pollen *n* a powder that flowers produce, which is carried by the wind or insects to other flowers so they can make seeds
rare *adj* not happening or seen very often
release *v* to let a person or animal go free
sanctuary *n* a safe area for birds or animals where people cannot hunt them
seed *n* a small grain that a new plant grows from
source *n* the place or thing that something comes from
Sumatran rhino *n* a rare hairy two-horned rhinoceros found in rainforests from Malaysia to Borneo
threat *n* someone or something that is in possible danger
tropical *adj* in or from the hottest or wettest parts of the world

Unit 6

Key vocabulary

article *n* a piece of writing in a newspaper or magazine
author *n* someone who writes a book

award *n* a prize given to someone or something
blog *n* a webpage in which you write about your opinions and what you have been doing
blogger *n* someone who writes a blog
character *n* a person in a book, play, film, etc.
concentrate *v* to think very carefully about what you are doing
content *n* the things that are written in a letter or book
critic *n* someone whose job is writing about music, movies, books, etc. and saying whether they are good or bad
entertaining *adj* interesting and enjoyable
fiction *n* books or stories about imaginary people and events
hilarious *adj* if something is hilarious, it is extremely funny and makes you laugh a lot
innovative *adj* new and better than in the past
inspire *v* to make you feel that you want to do or achieve something
magazine *n* a big thin publication with a paper cover that you can buy every week or month: magazines have news, stories, games, or pictures in them
metaphor *n* a way of describing something by comparing it to something else that it has similar qualities to, without using the words "like" or "as"
newspaper *n* pieces of thin paper that have news printed on them, that you can buy and read every day or every week
novel *n* a book in which the story, characters, and events are not real
plot *n* the story that is told in a book, movie, or play
poetry *v* poems in general
popular *adj* liked by a lot of people
post *n* a piece of writing on a blog
publish *v* to print a book, magazine, or newspaper and make it available for people to read and buy
writer *n* someone who writes

Unit 7
Key vocabulary

argument *n* a set of reasons that show that something is true or untrue, right or wrong etc
awkward *adj* embarrassing or difficult
behavior *n* the way that a person or animal behaves
collaborate *v* when one person or group collaborates with another, they work together
communicate *v* to talk to someone and tell them something
conversation *n* a talk between two or more people
convince *v* to make someone believe something
dishonest *adj* the quality of not being honest
emotional *adj* showing strong feelings to other people, especially by crying
express *v* to tell or show people what you think or feel
face-to-face *adj* if you come face to face with someone, you meet them and can talk to them or look at them directly

gesture *n* a movement of your hand, arms, or head that shows what you mean or how you feel
hearing *n* an opportunity to be heard
imitate *v* to copy the way a person or animal speaks or moves
message *v* to send a communication to another person
misunderstand *v* a to not understand a question, situation, or instructions correctly
non-verbal *adj* non-verbal communication consists of things, such as the expression on your face, your arm movements, or your tone of voice, which show how you feel about something without using words
persuade *v* to make someone decide to do something by giving him or her good reasons
represent *v* to speak for yourself or someone else in a trial or a court of law
request *v* to ask politely or formally
sign language *n* a language that uses hand movements and not words, used by some people who cannot hear
speechless *adj* unable to speak because you are too surprised
unfriendly *adj* not kind or friendly
written *adj* recorded in writing

Unit 8
Key vocabulary

attempt *v* to try to do something
bead *n* a small ball of plastic, wood, or glass with a hole in the middle, used for making jewelry
breeze *n* a gentle wind
carpentry *n* the skill or work of a carpenter, someone who makes wooden objects
chisel *n* a metal tool with a sharp flat end that you use to cut wood or stone
craft *n* a skilled activity in which you make something using your hands
drill *n* a tool or machine used for making holes in something hard
edge *n* the part of something that is farthest from the centre
embroidery *n* patterns or pictures that you sew on cloth as a decoration
expertly *adj* in a skilful way
file *v* to use a metal or wooden tool to rub something in order to make it smooth
flatten *v* to make something flat
fold *v* to bend a piece of paper or cloth so that one part covers another part
garment *n* a piece of clothing
hammer *v* to hit something with a hammer
homemade *adj* made at home rather than bought from the store
needle *n* a thin pointed piece of metal with a hole at one end for thread

saw *n* a tool that you use for cutting wood, with a flat blade and a row of sharp points
screw *v* to attach one thing to another with a screw
sculpture *n* an object made out of stone, wood, clay etc by an artist
sequin *n* a small shiny flat circle that is sewn on clothes for decoration
skilfully *v* doing very well
stitch *v* to sew two pieces of cloth together
upside-down *adj* with the top at the bottom and the bottom at the top

Unit 9
Key vocabulary

addict *n* a person who can't stop doing something
ascend *v* to go up
category *n* a group of similar people or things
cholesterol *n* a chemical found in your blood that can cause heart problems if you have too much of it
climbing *n* the sport of climbing mountains or large rocks
descend *v* to go down
energizing *adj* full of energy
glide *v* to move smoothly and quietly
member *n* someone who belongs to a group or organization
mountain biking *n* riding a bicycle with a strong frame and thick tires that can go over rough ground
paragliding *n* the sport of cross-country gliding using a specially designed parachute shaped like flexible wings
partner *n* someone with whom you do an activity that involves two people, such as dancing
player *n* someone who plays a game or a sport
plummet *v* to fall suddenly and quickly from a very high place
prize *n* something that is given to someone who is successful in a competition or race
program *n* a series of actions that are designed to achieve something important
race *n* a competition to find out who can do something fastest
reduce *v* to make something smaller or less than it was before
relaxing *adj* making you feel relaxed
scuba diving *n* the activity of swimming underwater using special breathing equipment
spiral *n* a curve that goes around a central point many times
skydiving *n* the sport of jumping from an airplane and falling through the sky before opening a parachute
triathlon *n* a sports competition in which you run, swim, and ride a bicycle
yoga *n* a set of exercises that relax your mind, keep your muscles strong, and help you bend your body easily

Unit 10
Key vocabulary

blizzard *n* a very bad storm with a lot of snow and wind
chairlift *n* a series of chairs suspended from a power-driven cable for conveying people, especially skiers, up a mountain
climate change *n* refers to changes in Earth's climate, especially the gradual rise in temperature caused by high levels of carbon dioxide and other gases
devastate *v* to damage something very badly
drought *n* a long period of dry weather when there is not enough rain
evaporate *v* if a liquid evaporates, it changes into steam or a gas
flood *n* a very large amount of water that flows onto and covers land that is usually dry
gifted *adj* having the natural ability to do something very well
global warming *n* a slight but continuing increase in the temperature of the lower atmosphere, usually attributed to an intensifying of the greenhouse effect that could lead to harmful climatic conditions
heat wave *n* some days or weeks when the weather is very hot
hurricane *n* a storm with very strong fast winds that comes from the ocean
intense *adj* having a very strong effect or felt very strongly
path *n* a track to walk through
period *n* a length of time with a beginning and an end
power lines *n* cables, especially above ground, along which electricity is passed to an area or building
resort *n* a place where a lot of people go for vacation
ski *v* to move down hills or across land in the snow, wearing skis
ski slope *n* a ski run of hard-packed snow
sled *n* something you sit or lie on to slide over snow
snowball *n* a ball that children make from snow and throw at each other
snowboard *v* a sport where you slide down a snow-covered hill on a large board
stranded *adj* not able to leave a place
stumble *v* to almost fall down while you are walking, especially if your foot hits something
typhoon *n* a violent tropical storm in the western part of the Pacific Ocean

Unit 11
Key vocabulary

bake *v* to cook something, such as bread or cake, in an oven
bunch *n* a group of things that grow together or are tied together, especially bananas, grapes, or flowers

chop *v* to cut food up with a knife
chopping board *n* a wooden or plastic board that you chop meat and vegetables on
condiment *n* a substance, such as salt, pepper, or mustard, that you add to food when you eat it in order to improve the flavor
dice *v* if you dice food, you cut it into small cubes
digest *v* when you digest food, it changes in your stomach into a form your body can use
edible *adj* safe to eat or good enough to eat
feast *n* a large meal for many people
fry *v* to cook something in hot oil or butter
frying pan *n* a round flat pan with a handle, used for frying food
grill *v* to cook by putting food on a flat metal frame with bars across it, above or below strong direct heat
ingredient *n* things that you use to make a particular food
meal *n* the food that you eat at a particular time
mix *v* to put different substances together to make something new
organic *adj* grown or produced without chemicals
raw *adj* not cooked
require *v* to need something
rotten *adj* rotten food or waste is old and starting to become soft because of natural chemical changes
saucepan *n* a deep metal container with a handle that you use for cooking
serving *n* an amount of food that is enough for one person
snack *n* something that you eat between meals
steam *v* to cook something with steam
texture *n* the way something feels when you touch it

Unit 12

Key vocabulary

abstract *adj* relating to idea rather than things you can see, hear, touch, or taste
annual *adj* happening every year
by heart *phrase* by or from memorization
calculus *n* a branch of advanced mathematics that deals with variable quantities
challenge *n* something difficult that needs skill or effort to do well
estimate *v* to calculate a number or amount approximately
manual *n* a book that tells you how to do something
memorize *v* to learn words, music, or facts so that you can remember them
mental *adj* relating to your thoughts or imagination
mind *n* your thoughts or the part of your brain you use for thinking and imagining things
prepare *v* to make something ready
random *adj* happening or chosen without any plan or pattern
recall *n* the ability to something from the past

repetition *n* the act of saying and doing the same thing again, or doing it many times
research *n* a study of a subject in order to find out new information
revise *v* to study, as for an exam
rote *n* to learn something by repeating it until you remember it
set goals *phrase* the process of identifying something that you want to accomplish and establishing measurable goals and timeframes
stimulus *n* something that causes something else to happen, develop, or react
study *v* to spend time going to classes, reading, etc. to learn about a subject
symmetrical *adj* to have two sides of something that are exactly the same
system *n* an organized set of ideas or methods
take notes *phrase* write down so as to remember
technique *n* a special way of doing something